Newcomers
in an
Ancient
Land

Newcomers
in an
Ancient
Land

ADVENTURES, LOVE, AND
SEEKING MYSELF IN 1960s ISRAEL

PAULA WAGNER

SHE WRITES PRESS

בָּרוּךְ אַתָּה יְיָ אֱלֹהֵינוּ מֶלֶךְ הָעוֹלָם, שֶׁהֶחֱיָנוּ וְקִיְּמָנוּ
וְהִגִּיעָנוּ לַזְּמַן הַזֶּה.

Baruch atah, Adonai Eloheinu, Melech haolam,

shehecheyanu, v'kiy'manu, v'higiyanu laz'man hazeh.

Blessed are You, Adonai our God, Sovereign of the universe, who has

created us and sustained us, and brought us to this day.

Published July 2019
Printed in the United States of America
Print ISBN: 978-1-63152-529-2
E-ISBN: 978-1-63152-530-8
Library of Congress Control Number: 2019902942

For information, address:
She Writes Press
1569 Solano Ave #546
Berkeley, CA 94707

Interior design by Tabitha Lahr

She Writes Press is a division of SparkPoint Studio, LLC.

Names and identifying characteristics have been changed to protect the privacy of certain individuals.

For my mother Jean, who shared her love of language and believed I could write.

For my father Leon, whose Jewish heritage set me on a lifelong journey.

CONTENTS

PART III: ENGLAND—SUMMER 1964

PART IV: ISRAEL—FALL 1964

Introduction:

SUNRISE OVER THE GOLAN

I crept along a dirt road under a black dome studded with stars on my way to my job as a volunteer in the vineyards of Kibbutz Dan. At four in the morning, only the chirping of crickets and the crunch of my work boots broke the peace along this deserted stretch of the pre-1967 border between Israel and Syria. Until the rest of the work crew arrived at six, I would be alone. Or would I?

DANGER, EXPLOSIVES, KEEP OUT warned the faded signs in Hebrew, English, and Arabic on a haphazard barricade of rusty barbed wire, broken concrete, thorn trees, and weeds. From just beyond, I could hear a faint braying, and I caught a glimpse of something white and flowing. A parachute? My heart pounded and my red hair stood on end as adrenaline surged through every cell in my eighteen-year-old body. But on closer inspection, it was only the billowing jellaba of a Syrian farmer tilling his fields with a hand-held plow drawn by a recalcitrant donkey. Such a biblical vision made it hard to imagine that conflict still racked this ancient land.

One by one, the stars winked out, the sky turned pale, and a rosy glow backlit the massive shoulders of the Syrian hills hunched over the valley. I knew those silhouetted hills hid bunkers; and in those bunkers crouched soldiers; and in the crosshairs of their Kalashnikovs, I could be a target. Yet for a moment, a wild part of me dared imagine that the sight of a naïve young girl in khaki shorts and shirt might offer a welcome distraction from the tedium of war.

By now, opalescent clouds of apricot, lavender, and magenta were gathering at fever speed. Just when it seemed the light could get no brighter, a blinding fireball burst over the mountains. Quaking in my boots, yet quivering with delight, I stood transfixed by the beauty and danger of this ancient land in which I was a newcomer.

The Israel that greeted me on that distant, dusty road no longer exists except in memory. Today, parts of the Promised Land have been paved over to such an extent that the life and landscape of the early sixties in this story may sound fantastical. Humming freeways carry a population of nine million between skyscrapers and shopping malls. Villages have become towns and towns have burgeoned into cities in a building frenzy designed to accommodate a population that has tripled in half a century. Jerusalem, while officially united, remains a tale of two cities deeply divided, East and West.

Of course, I too have grown and changed from a teenager whose life was practically a blank slate into a professional woman, wife, mother, grandmother, writer, and more. But back then, Israel and I were in many ways coming of age like a pair of adolescents (we had, after all, come into being only three years apart). In that sense, the country's cocky *chutzpah* and can-do attitude were a good match for my own mix of idealism and bravado. If the country's pioneering spirit inspired me, my post-war generation was a source of hope and renewal for Israel after the Holocaust.

But the country's heady idealism was not shared by all. As I was falling in love with my adoptive homeland, I was barely aware that Palestinians were grieving the loss of theirs. What Israelis called the War of Independence, they called the *Naqba*—a national disaster that had driven them into squalid refugee camps in an unwelcoming diaspora. But after two thousand years of exile and persecution, the new Jewish inhabitants had little sympathy for the misfortunes of Palestinian refugees. While ordinary citizens on both sides longed for peace, security and geopolitical issues beyond their control increasingly overshadowed their desires. Although it would still be several years before the War of 1967 launched the ongoing occupation of Palestinian lands outside Israel's recognized borders, the clouds of conflict were never far from the horizon.

However, this book is not meant to romanticize, politicize, rationalize past or present affairs, but to tell the story of a personal journey that came to determine the course of my life, though I had no idea of this at the time. I went to Israel in search of a closer understanding of my father through his Jewish roots, but planted my own roots there instead. Not only was I leaving my small hometown, I was also leaving my mother for a foreign land, just as she had left hers. On top of this, I was struggling to become an individual, distinct from my identical twin. Lurching on the tightrope between fear and the urge for independence, I plunged into the future with all the inexorable momentum of youth. That quest has now become a reverse journey through the arc of time, connecting the young girl I was with the woman I have become.

I have tried hard to render all the events, people, and places in this book to the best of my memory, research, and intuition. But memories can be like snowflakes, distinct yet quickly dissolving on the wavy mirror of the mind. Even shared memories within a family can be wildly dissonant. So who is to say what is strictly true? I only know my words to be "truly true" when they resonate in my heart like a well-struck gong or the solid crack of a baseball bat on a home run.

PART I

ISRAEL—FALL 1963

Chapter 1

SETTING SAIL

Walking a gangplank, cutting the cord
Sailing the sea to an unknown shore

Whump! The New York Port Authority Customs Agent stamped my passport photo, raising an inky welt like a slap in the face. Next in line, my twin sister Naomi presented hers. Squinting, the agent swiveled his head from one of us to the other in a double take.

"Didn't I just stamp your passport, young lady?"

"No sir, that was my sister's," Naomi replied. We were used to the twin drill. Still perplexed, he finally stamped her photo with an identical welt.

"Even with wrinkled faces, people still can't tell us apart," I groaned as we got in line to board the *Theodore Herzl*.

"Maybe that's how we'll look when we're old enough to write our memoirs," joked Naomi, pretending to hobble up the gangplank.

At the age of eighteen, old age was as unimaginable to me as infinity. But whatever lay ahead, I hoped it would be exciting enough to write about when I got there.

On October 19, 1963, Naomi and I were on our way to Israel to study Hebrew in a program called an *ulpan* and work on a collective farm called a *kibbutz*. But now that my urge to explore my Jewish roots was becoming a reality, it felt like a one-way passage through uncharted waters. I felt seasick just standing on the dock.

Now a large gate clanged shut as if to seal off my childhood behind me. Meanwhile, the sailors herded us up the gangplank with the other passengers. There was no time to look over my shoulder with regret like Lot's wife in the Old Testament. Only the future mattered now.

"*Kadima, kadima,*" (move along) shouted the sailors.

Before its recent conversion to carry passengers, the *Theodore Herzl* had been a cargo vessel. With our limited budgets, flying had been out of the question. But the glossy *Zim Lines* brochure had made the seventeen-day voyage across the Atlantic and Mediterranean look as inviting as a cruise. So why were the rough and tumble stevedores not behaving like white-gloved waiters?

"This feels like *Exodus,*" muttered Naomi.

"Yeah, like the ancient Hebrews fleeing Egypt," I added as the gangplank buckled beneath my feet, almost pitching me into the sludgy harbor below. I grabbed the swaying guide rope for balance, but the rough yet slippery fibers ripped my palms raw. "Ouch!" I yelped.

The exhausting two-week trip from San Francisco to the East Coast by Greyhound Bus was finally catching up with me. Schlepping my heavy pack and dodging midnight gropers in grimy bus terminals hadn't been as romantic as I'd imagined. Having risen at dawn for the last leg of the trip from Philadelphia to New York, my arms ached and my head throbbed. The sheen on my dreams was wearing thin.

No sooner had I reached the upper deck than a sailor took one look at our tickets and jerked his thumb downward toward a rusty metal staircase.

"Your cabin is down below."

"Phew, what stinks?" asked Naomi as we spiraled down two levels.

"And what's that deafening noise?"

The floor vibrated under our feet with a thunderous roar, while the putrid odor of diesel fumes and stale urine filled our noses.

We stared incredulously at the door with our number on it.

"These are our, uh, quarters?" Naomi quipped. But I was not amused.

In my fantasies, I had imagined myself rocking in a cradle as I crossed the ocean, not swallowed up like Jonah in the belly of this belching beast. Located squarely between the roaring engine room to one side and leaky toilets on the other, our third-class cabin was in the bowels of the ship.

"Guess we'll be spending a lot of time above deck," I gasped, but the noise and stench drowned out my words. Tossing our bags on the narrow bunk beds, we rushed back up the rickety staircase just as the ship nosed out of the harbor.

"How on earth will we survive like this for seventeen days?" we moaned in unison. I'd kept the promise I'd made at fifteen to make this trip, but now I wondered what the Promised Land would deliver.

Shadows lengthened across the deck as the sun set over the rusty scow that would be our home for the next three weeks. Unsure whether to laugh or cry, Naomi and I clung to each other as the darkening sky and water slowly swallowed up the land.

"Oh well, seventeen days in this clink will give us plenty of time to think," Naomi rhymed.

"Or die in the stink," I retorted.

"I'm starving. Let's get us some vittles."

"Not sprinkled with spittle!"

"Oh cease!" I cried. "In seventeen days we'll be utterly crazed!"

Spontaneous rhyming was a favorite pastime that always lightened our mood, but it was hard to stop once we got going. We made our way to the mess hall for a surprisingly tasty supper of crispy pan-fried chicken breasts called *schnitzel*, roasted potatoes, and a tomato/cucumber salad. Exhausted, I fell asleep not long after dinner, the incessant drone of the engines drowning out my dreams.

At breakfast the following morning, we shared a table with an Israeli man in khaki pants and a casual shirt open at the neck. As soon as he learned we were going to study Hebrew, he insisted on giving us a lesson over our soft-boiled eggs, thick slices of brown bread and butter, various cheeses, yogurt, tomatoes, cucumbers, and pickled herring.

"*Bruchim ha'ba'im! Baruch Ha'Shem!*" (Welcome, God be praised!) We did our best to repeat the phrase.

"Good. Now enjoy a typical Israeli breakfast," he said. "The herring is especially tasty, but watch out for the tiny bones."

To please him, I took a slimy bite and gulped it down with my tea.

The man laughed. But his smile faded at the taste of his soft-boiled eggs.

"These eggs are cold," he complained, summoning the waiter.

"So what?" snapped the waiter with an insolent smirk.

Instantly, a shouting match began until suddenly, the waiter grabbed another egg from the table, tucking it between his legs with a suggestive gesture and more rapid-fire Hebrew. But instead of the outrage I expected, the passenger burst out laughing as if the sailor had told an off-color joke.

"What on earth was that all about?" I asked as soon as the sailor took his leave.

"Ah," chuckled the man, "I'm embarrassed to tell you. But in Hebrew the word for eggs—*baetzim*—is also, how can I say, uh . . . slang for a man's balls. So when I said my eggs were cold, the waiter asked if he should warm them up between his legs. Now you'll never forget this important lesson, I'm sure!"

Until that moment, I had revered Hebrew as a sacred language. But if these two men were any indication, the daily modern version had taken a turn for the profane.

After breakfast I went on deck for some desperately needed fresh air. The morning was mild for mid-October, and the sea was a calm gray-green. A pale band of clouds trailed the ship's wake. Nursing the remains of my tea, I let my memory of the past six months unspool:

May—leaving home on the day after high school graduation and steeling my heart as my mother waved and wept from the doorstep; June—landing a summer job in San Francisco; August—receiving my passport; September—buying a bus ticket and boat fare; October—rumbling across the country on the Greyhound to board this ship. Yet everything that had led up to this moment now seemed to belong to another lifetime.

I tossed the dregs of my tea overboard and watched them float briefly on the foam before vanishing into the waves, exactly like my previous life. Yet the comforting taste lingered on my tongue, a bittersweet reminder of the countless cups of tea my mother had poured me as I was growing up.

As a young woman, my mother had made her own Atlantic crossing to bring Naomi and me to America from her birthplace, and ours, in London. She and Dad had met in the midst of World War II, when he was an American GI stationed in Britain. Despite the chaos and carnage of war, they had managed to fall in love. But for my mother, the marriage had meant leaving her own mother behind. As I grew up, Mom had never much mentioned that fateful decision, and I'd learned not to ask. Instead, she'd adapted to her new life in the US with a grace and courage I had taken for granted. Now a wave of empathy engulfed me, and my tears fell into the sea—"as if it needed more salt," she would have said. Had my mother also felt the poignant mix of elation and dread that I felt now, as she too sailed toward an unknown future? My mother often said with an air of fateful resignation that her "life just happened" to her. Despite her training at the prestigious London School of Speech and Drama, World War II had dashed her starry dreams of acting on the London stage. Instead, she'd married and become the mother of twins, then immigrated to America. Two momentous years from 1944–46 had forever altered the course of my mother's life. But headstrong and idealistic, I was determined to *make my own life happen*!

*Jean and Leon with newborns Paula &
Naomi, London 1945*

*My own voyage on the Theodore Herzl
wasn't nearly as romantic as this
vintage poster for Zim Lines.*

Chapter 2

ESTHER: A CHARISMATIC MENTOR

If Israel was our boldest adventure yet, it was by no means the first for Naomi and me. By the time we were ten, we had traveled from England to Texas, Iowa, and Kansas before our family finally settled in Arcata, a remote logging and fishing town with a small state college on the coast of Northern California. With each move, we had adapted like tumbleweeds to new schools, friends, and neighborhoods, only to be uprooted once again. Crossing the Atlantic at age four to visit our mother's family in England, my clearest memory is of the Feins, an Israeli family on board who also had identical twin daughters. At fourteen, Naomi and I had returned to London once again for a year of boarding school at Channing School for Girls, this time without our family.

Initially, we struggled to surmount the steep academic learning curve and loneliness of boarding school. In our scratchy rust-brown uniforms with matching berets and ties, we felt like prisoners, allowed out on Saturday afternoons only as far as the local sweet shop. We could visit our newfound aunts, uncles, and cousins only during the holidays, but to reach their welcoming arms meant navigating the London Tube and daunting trains on our own.

For the first time in our lives, Naomi and I needed each other in a way we never had at home, where we had been more likely to compete than to cooperate. Without the ability to communicate via cell phones or internet in those days, we were forced to face our problems alone. While incredibly challenging, my year in England forced me to develop a level of maturity beyond my years. Though I greatly missed my parents and younger siblings, Jonathan and Laura, I learned I could survive without them.

But returning to fog-bound Arcata—population 5,235 in 1960—was an exercise in reverse culture shock. After the initial joy of reuniting with friends and family, my parents' rules soon chafed like an outgrown sweater. I couldn't imagine how I'd survive three more years until high school graduation. As a teenager, babysitting was the only job I could get, but just when my desperation hit bottom, it became my salvation.

"Are you available next Thursday?" asked a voice with an unfamiliar accent.

"Thank you for coming," said the tall woman when I arrived. She wore a caftan of diagonal red-and-black stripes that set off her olive skin and angular frame. Her name was Esther.

Gold hoops glowed in her long dark hair, and a warm smile softened her beaky nose. Crossing her threshold, I entered a living room of colorful wall hangings accented by glowing copper. A savory aroma wafted from the kitchen.

Esther poured two gold-rimmed glasses of fresh mint tea and set them on a low brass tray. Although I loved my mother's milky English tea, the mint was heavenly.

"Please," she offered, "let's just get to know each other a little. I'm not actually going anywhere today." Most of my babysitting clients were only too eager to leave me with their charges. But Esther took her time.

"Daniel, come meet Paula," she called to her tousled three-year-old son, playing on a woven rug. "She'll be taking care of you when I'm busy." The boy looked up briefly before continuing to rev his toy airplanes as if launching them from a magic carpet.

If this was an interview, it felt relaxing. I too wanted to ask a million questions of this charismatic woman. Where was she from and how had she come to live in Arcata? Over the steaming tea, she began her story: She was originally from Morocco but had immigrated to Israel when she was young.

"After my own university studies, I married an American professor. That's how I came here. He was just hired in the English department at HSU—Humboldt State University."

"My dad teaches in the Music Department," I interjected. "My sister Naomi and I babysit for almost all the faculty families." So that's how she'd found me—through the faculty network.

In the coming months, I would learn more of Esther's story. Along with virtually the entire Moroccan Jewish community, her family had left for Israel in the early 1950s, draining Morocco of doctors, teachers, lawyers, businessmen, and entire villages.

"We went to Israel to help build the new country—but ironically, we weren't well received when we arrived. The European Jews who were already there—the *Ashkenazim*—thought we *Sephardic* Jews from North Africa were uncivilized. It's true we had different traditions, but to them, we were only fit for raising chickens! Even though I spoke four languages—English, French, Hebrew, and Arabic—I still didn't feel respected." Her voice rose with ire.

"Now I'm stuck in this tiny town with a three-year-old. In a big city, I could be a French pastry chef or an interpreter. But there is no market for those talents here."

Pausing to reflect, she fixed her large dark eyes on me. "You have your whole life ahead of you. Don't let anything hold you back!"

In fact, Esther may have been barely ten years my senior, perhaps in her midtwenties. But an invisible bond of solidarity soon bridged our differences. Ambitious and charming, Esther had looked to America for opportunity. Now her plan had apparently stalled. Clearly, she considered Arcata a backwater, despite the melancholy beauty of its craggy beaches and towering redwoods.

Each time we met, our friendship deepened as we compared differences and shared aspirations. While my family was secular and unaffiliated with the Jewish community—we celebrated only the major Jewish holidays like Chanukah and Passover—Esther came from a traditionally observant background. I knew next to nothing about Israel, but her descriptions fascinated me. Transcending her personal experience, she described the challenges of a young socialist nation rising from the ashes of the Holocaust. The seeds she planted fell in the fertile soil of my adolescent idealism and soon germinated. I yearned to identify with a community whose beliefs I shared. Despite its problems—including the conflicts with its Arab neighbors—which Esther neither glorified nor minimized, Israel was a land where young people could make a difference.

One especially gloomy day, Esther mentioned a work/study program or ulpan where students could learn Hebrew while volunteering on a collective farm called a kibbutz.

"That sounds exciting," I sputtered. The more she described, the more captivated I became.

"Maybe you could go after college," she suggested.

As if she had handed me a magic key, my heart sprang at the idea. But how could I possibly wait that long?

"What about going *before* college?" I ventured.

She took some time before responding. "Well, I don't see why not. The work isn't easy, but they always need young people. Lots of European kids do go between high school and college."

The ulpan appeared to offer a solution to my wanderlust

that was both ideal and practical. I decided then and there to find my way to Israel as soon as I finished high school. If I could survive away from home at age fourteen, I could certainly do so at eighteen. As I headed home in high spirits that afternoon, the coastal fog lifted, revealing a horizon as boundless as the vision I would nurture to fruition over the coming three years.

Although I was an A student in high school, the hands-on work/study program would offer a welcome break from classroom learning as well as the chance to pursue my love of languages. After my year in England, I'd gained a much fuller understanding of my mother's culture. Now it made sense to explore my father's Jewish roots, however distant and deeply they were buried. Only secretly did I dare to hope that in Israel I might find the key to his elusive heart.

Despite my growing independence from Naomi, I wasn't ready to go so far away without her. But when I first broached the idea, she was skeptical. For months we argued the pros and cons of the trip like two tightrope walkers in a tug of war.

"C'mon, it'll be an *adventure*," I cajoled, invoking our childhood watchword.

I reinforced my case with glossy brochures from Ha'Shomer Ha'Tzair, the left-wing youth movement, showing "young pioneers" happily picking oranges, driving tractors, and excavating precious archaeological artifacts in the desert. Naomi's resistance only strengthened my resolve until eventually she relented. Once united, we poured our energy into planning all the details. Earning enough money would be our biggest challenge. With no work but babysitting in our neck of the woods, we would need to get summer jobs in San Francisco after high school to supplement our savings.

When the time came to tell our parents, I dreaded their reaction. Seated at the head of the table for a family meeting, Dad flared his ample nostrils—a familiar sign of disapproval that Naomi and I referred to as the *Big Sniff*. Mom poured tea to ease the tension, her solution for all occasions. After listening to our plans, Dad flared his nose again. A long and awkward hush fell over the room.

"Well, girls, that doesn't sound very realistic," he pronounced at last.

"Don't you think it's a shame not to use your scholarship to UC Berkeley, Paula?" added Mom in a tone that filled me with guilt, although I'd anticipated the question.

"Don't worry," I answered confidently. "I already contacted the university. They say I can defer it for a year. Besides, think how much more I'll be learning than I could ever learn in a classroom!"

But Dad had more objections. "And exactly how will you finance this, uh . . . jaunt?"

I'd been prepared for Mom's guilt attack, but not Dad's sarcasm. In his eyes, the plan was absurd, our babysitting money was paltry, and our prospects for finding jobs in San Francisco virtually nil with only a high school education. Under his calm but withering logic, my dreams shrank until I felt as small as Alice in Wonderland. But what had I expected? Dad liked to be in control. And here I was challenging his authority by proposing to escape to the far side of the world! Ever since Naomi and I were young, whenever we acted up, Dad would order us to *act more grown up*. But now he seemed unable or unwilling to acknowledge that, in fact, we *had* grown up.

Like an archer's fist, my heart tightened as I let fly the last arrow in my quiver, aiming straight for Dad.

"I thought maybe you'd *approve* of us going to Israel," I ventured. "After all, you *are* Jewish, aren't you?"

My arrow hit Dad's sore spot squarely at the core of his being, the place where he tried to keep his ambivalence about his Jewish identity hidden. He flinched. In my zeal to protect my dreams, I saw how much I'd hurt him. After another excruciating pause, he simply turned his palms upward in a gesture of surrender.

"Well girls, if it's only a year, and if Paula stays with our old friends the Feins, and Naomi stays nearby, then I guess I can't stand in your way."

The resignation in his sad brown eyes and voice seemed to well up from deep in his soul. He had always taught us to challenge authority with a capital A—as long as it wasn't *his* authority. I had won my freedom, but had I lost my dad? As I'd grown older, we'd both grown more distant. Now the fun we'd shared when I was a little girl seemed to recede like laughter from a deserted playground.

After this conversation, Dad made no further resistance. But neither did he offer any encouragement, advice, or financial support. Perhaps he and Mom simply hoped our harebrained scheme would blow over.

However, as graduation approached in the spring of 1963, my anticipation and doubts grew in equal measure. What if my parents were right—what if I was planning to drop off the edge of the earth? What about my scholarship to UCB? And what would I be missing? The Civil Rights Movement and antiwar protests of the sixties were still nascent, but I could feel them rumbling below the surface. Their growing energy was palpable at the American Friends Service Committee (AFSC) youth conferences I had begun to attend in the Bay Area. If I went to Israel, I'd miss all that. But I could not regret what I did not yet know.

Chapter 3

A FANTASTICAL FAREWELL

B y the fall of 1963, Naomi and I had finally saved enough
money to reach New York and Haifa. We wouldn't need
much once we got to Israel. As a farewell, we planned to spend
our last night with our mentor Esther, who now lived in Philadelphia. It seemed only fitting to thank her for her inspiration
and support. The next morning we'd catch our last bus to the
New York Port Authority at five o'clock. But Esther's fantastical
send-off almost cost us the trip.

She was thrilled to see us. "We *must* celebrate with a
special meal at my favorite Moroccan restaurant!" she exclaimed,
promptly calling a sitter.

At the entrance, a mustachioed maître d' welcomed us
warmly. He and Esther exchanged three kisses on each cheek
in the Moroccan tradition.

Inside, I'd never seen such sumptuous décor. From high
on the ceiling, huge chandeliers sparkled over a sea of silver-
ware and ruby lamps on white tablecloths. Thick gold cords
held back velveteen drapes at vaulted windows. Somewhere
out of sight, a woman sang in a sultry minor key to the beat of
a hand drum.

Soon, plates of hummus, pita bread, and olives appeared, while Esther ordered main dishes of succulent lamb, chicken, and steaming vegetables served over mountains of couscous, spiced with cumin and turmeric. Midway through the meal, Esther pricked up her ears at the sound of four businessmen at the table behind us chatting in Arabic.

"Pardon me, gentlemen," she murmured, catching their attention with her kohl-rimmed eyes. "I couldn't help wondering if you are from my hometown of Marrakech?"

"But of course!" they answered, delighted to meet a compatriot.

By the time we'd finished our dessert of flaky baklava and tiny cups of Turkish coffee, the men were insisting that we accompany them back to their villa on the outskirts of Philadelphia.

Cupping his hand to Esther's ear, her husband, Richard, protested. "We don't even know these guys, and it's already late. What about the sitter and the girls' bus at five?"

"But it's an insult to refuse their hospitality," argued Esther, invoking the sacred rules of Middle Eastern etiquette. "Especially since I made the first move."

Taking Esther and Naomi with them, the men tore out of the parking lot, down dark alleys and onto the turnpike, with Richard and me in hot pursuit. After what seemed like forever, the silver Mercedes swerved suddenly onto a long tree-lined side road before finally slowing at a pair of wrought-iron gates.

Ushering us into their large private mansion, our hosts smiled graciously before disappearing to prepare some drinks. Glancing around in disbelief, I saw rich Persian rugs covering the floors and stern-faced Middle Eastern potentates staring down from the walls. Each gilded frame bore a name like King Abdullah of Saudi Arabia, King Hussein of Jordan, King Hassan II of Morocco, and members of the infamous Assad family of Syria. The *Arabian Nights* had nothing on this.

Our hosts soon returned bearing large red goblets.

"Just *pretend*," breathed Richard. "You have no idea what's in these drinks." Luckily the opaque glass obscured the contents as we feigned small sips. Just then a grandfather clock bonged twice.

"We really must go," said Esther. "The young ladies have a five o'clock bus to catch."

"But where are they going? Why not stay overnight?" our hosts persisted.

Desperate to escape without mentioning Israel, the sworn enemy of its Arab neighbors, we sputtered our regrets and hurried out into the waning night.

After barely two hours of restless sleep, the alarm jolted me awake. I nudged Naomi and rose quietly. Unshaven and haggard, Richard drove us to the Philadelphia station.

"Take care!" he cautioned, hugging us goodbye at the cavernous entrance. Shivering in the predawn chill, I returned his wishes as warmly as I could.

"Give our love to Esther."

Under the yellow glare of the street lamps, the city of brotherly love looked littered and forlorn. Naomi and I rode the last leg of our overland journey in numbed exhaustion.

Chapter 4

"GINGIT!"

"*Gingit, gingit!*" shouted the sailors, going wild at the sight of our bright red hair and identical looks whenever Naomi or I poked our heads up on deck.

It didn't take long to learn that *gingit* meant redhead, a derivation of the English nickname *ginger*, just as we'd been called in London.

Would we never escape their hounding? Like hungry alley cats, the sailors chased us over the decks and through the rigging in hopes of cornering us for a kiss.

"Kiss me and I'll let you go," they teased as we struggled against their strong tattooed arms. Stevedores by trade, they hated their new roles as bellboys now that their ship carried passengers instead of cargo. We did our best to outsmart their advances, but appeasement was often our only means of freedom. Yet even the smallest concession of a peck on the cheek would make the sailors clamor for more. To survive, we stuck together, leaving our cabin only for meals or when the steamy stench became unbearable.

Still, I couldn't resist the beauty of the nocturnal sky. Leaving Naomi below late one evening, I crept up on deck alone. The scene that greeted me made me forget all about the sailors. High over the cobalt sea, a shimmering canopy of stars arched all the way down to the horizon like a fishnet tugged by unseen hands. Flying fish played in the ship's wake, their silvery tails and bellies twisting and flashing in the starlight. Leaning over the stern, I let the salt spray wash over my face. Time stood still, as boundless as eternity. Only the low thrum of the engines, the slapping of the blue-black waves, and the starry dome overhead reminded me I was still on Planet Earth. As I watched in awe, a poem that had won me first place in my third-grade class in Iowa floated into the net of my memory:

> *Sailing boat, sailing boat, sailing away*
> *Over the ocean and far away*
> *Will you come back or will you stay there?*
> *Where will you go? Where, where, where?*

Had the mention of an ocean somehow set it apart from the cows and cornfields in my classmates' poems?

This journey begged the question once again: where did I belong? Where was home? Perhaps I wasn't charting my own course after all. Maybe I was following in my mother's footsteps by leaving her just as she had left her mother. Now Naomi and I would be the second generation of daughters to leave our mother for a foreign land.

But a shadow slinking up behind me suddenly interrupted my reverie.

"Gingit," it hissed.

Quick as a mouse, I scurried across the deck and disappeared down the spiral staircase to the safety of my berth below. The pungent dungeon was better than a nocturnal confrontation with my tormentor.

I banged on the door to our cabin with my fists, shouting for Naomi to open up. She didn't need to ask to know I was escaping a sailor. I flopped down on my bunk, heaving for breath.

"One more week and we'll be off this floating flophouse," was all she said.

Indeed, this would be our final night on the Atlantic after ten long days at sea. The next morning, the *Theodore Herzl* would pass through the Straits of Gibraltar and into the Mediterranean. If only I could get some sleep, I hoped to see the mighty Rock of Gibraltar at sunrise.

Our final week also promised a brief reprieve off ship in the form of a one-day stop on the island of Rhodes and two days in the Greek port of Piraeus. I wasn't the only passenger dying to set foot on terra firma. For days, the ship's dining room had been buzzing in anticipation of the excursion to Rhodes' famous Valley of the Butterflies. The velvety golden-brown insects were fabled to cling to your clothes and hair as you hiked through their gum tree habitat. After Rhodes, we'd have two full days in Athens to explore the ancient Greek city and the Parthenon. A mere two days later, we would dock in Haifa at dawn!

Chapter 5

DAD AND AVRAM:

TWO JEWS, TEN OPINIONS

As the seventeen-day passage drew to a welcome end, I felt a surge of excitement tinged with fear displacing my long-nurtured dream. What would life on Kibbutz Ein Hashofet be like? Would I recognize my hosts, the Feins, whom I remembered only from my parents' stories of how our families had met on another Atlantic crossing so long ago? A photo from that trip shows Naomi and me snuggled between another pair of twins—Ruth and Naomi Fein. Their long dark braids look untouched by the salty spray whipping through our unruly red curls. I did a mental calculation. The Fein sisters would now be twenty-three, but in my memory, they remained forever nine.

Now the sea spray showering over the deck of the Theodore Herzl teased my memories of that trip back to life.

"Remember when we flapped our arms in the wind and pretended to be seagulls on the *Mauritania*?" I asked, hoping she too recalled how we'd swooped across the slippery deck, arms outstretched.

"Caw, caw!" she crowed in an exuberant child's voice.

Our family and the Feins had met by sheer happenstance fourteen years earlier when Naomi and I were only four. While lining up to board the *Mauritania* for our first visit back to London, a murmur had rippled through the crowd: "Did you see those *two* twins—no, did you see those *four* twins?" Naomi and I usually ignored the attention attracted by our identical curly red mops, but this time *another* set of identical girls with dark brown braids stood directly behind us!

"Dad," I whispered, "look at those girls behind us." Dad glanced in the direction of the family behind us, then turned to introduce us.

"I see we appear to have something in common," he quipped. "I'm Leon Wagner, this is my wife, Jean, and these are our daughters, Naomi and Paula."

"*Plis to mit you,*" came the heavily accented answer. "I'm Avram Fein, and this my wife, Frieda, and our girls, Naomi and Ruth."

"Well, we have even more in common than I thought with two Naomis, a Ruth, and a Paula," my mother said with a laugh. But I squirmed at the sound of my name. Why couldn't my parents have given *me* a biblical name like my sister? But at the same time, I was glad they hadn't called me Ruth, a name I liked no better than my own. Maybe in Israel I'd find a new Hebrew name, as many people did there. But try as I might, no other name felt or sounded quite right.

The handshakes between the Feins and my parents that day would launch an enduring friendship. With my arrival in Israel, that relationship was about to take another turn. Much as my parents had worried, they'd been reassured by the Feins' invitation for me to stay on their kibbutz. Meanwhile, Naomi would stay nearby on Kibbutz Hazorea.

Over the course of that first transatlantic voyage, Naomi and I had explored the *Mauritania* with our newfound friends who were supposed to be keeping an eye on us while our mothers enjoyed a rare chance to read uninterrupted, and Dad and Avram carried on deep conversations without end.

Later I would learn that the Feins were on their way home to Israel following a three-year stint in the US, where Avram had worked as a *shaleach*, a recruiter for the *Ha'Shomer Ha'Tzair* kibbutz movement. Short and square, he may have been forty, but his graying hair made him appear older, although to my child's eyes, all grown-ups looked ancient. Avram was Polish but had immigrated to Palestine before World War II to become one of the founders of Kibbutz Ein Hashofet in 1937, then fought in Israel's War of Independence in 1948. Staunchly committed to the secular, socialist, and collective ideals of Zionism in that era, he was part of the Pioneer generation called *chalutzim*.

Despite his heavy Polish accent, Avram was as talkative as Frieda was quiet. Naomi and Ruth spoke fluent Hebrew and English, a feat I both envied and admired, and which made me yearn to learn another language too. Why not, when they made it seem so easy? It was my first exposure to another language, and the new sounds and rhythms made my brain dance!

Of course, at age four, I couldn't possibly have understood Dad and Avram's deck chair conversations that summer of 1949, but from their tone of voice, they sounded quite serious. Dad was always telling Naomi and me to watch our tone of voice when we got snarky, but this was somehow different. Years later, I realized that Avram had been pouring his considerable powers of persuasion into recruiting our family to come to Israel and join his kibbutz. I imagined the conversation going something like this:

"Leon, you should bring your family to visit our kibbutz! Ve haf everything you need—free healthcare, education, and a wonderful sense of community. Besides, Israel *needs* people like you to help realize the socialist dream!"

But for Dad, an assimilated political lefty who felt American first and Jewish second, Avram's logic was tantalizing yet troublesome. Caught between his lofty political ideals and his desire to expand beyond the confines of Jewish life, Dad felt ambivalent.

"Thanks, Avram. You make kibbutz life sound amazing. But what would a nonpracticing Jewish college music professor like me do in Israel—much less my non-Jewish wife?"

"Ah, no problem," answered Avram. "*Ve haf a soluuuu-tion*! You and your wife spend six months in an ulpan—a work-study program—learning the language, getting used to our system. After that, you can both work on the kibbutz." Avram had a soluuuu-tion for everything.

"But what kind of work would we do?"

"Why, you can teach music, and Jean can teach English at our regional high school. Ve haf lots of cultural activities on our kibbutz. Almost everyone plays an instrument or sings. We value the arts as much as physical labor, but of course, it's more important to put the good of the group over your own individual desires."

Dad didn't mind physical labor; in fact, he respected it. He supported unions and had later pushed to unionize university professors in California. At home, he was always refinishing old pieces of furniture or working in his garden.

"But what about the girls—what would they do?" he continued.

"They can live in the children's house," answered Avram without missing a beat. "Trust me, your kids will learn Hebrew *chik chak*—in no time. And Israel has the best education in the world. As for Jean, Frieda tells me she doesn't really like to cook. So . . . she'd never haf to cook another meal in collective dining room!"

"Well, that's true." Dad couldn't help but laugh. I loved whatever Mom cooked and wolfed it down voraciously. But Mom would much rather have been producing a play than putting three meals a day on the table.

"But Avram, I just don't know how Jean would fit in," Dad continued. "After all, she's not Jewish."

"No problem," answered Avram. "She can convert."

But Avram's soluuuu-tion struck Dad like a thunderclap.

"What, convert?" he growled. "I thought you detested those old rabbis like I do, Avram. Do you want Israel to be a theocracy or a democracy?"

"Calm down, Leon. You don't have to *believe* all that religious mumbo jumbo, but you know as well as I do if your wife converted, it vould be easier for everyone, especially your girls. They vould haf a clear identity—not half and half."

Dad took a deep breath, struggling to regain his composure, but his nostrils still flared, a sure sign of consternation. Avram had touched a raw nerve.

"Well, Avram, I have to disagree. I can teach my girls all the Jewish values they need without the sanction of official Judaism. I'm sorry, but they will just have to figure out their identities for themselves."

My need to trace this contradiction to its roots was exactly why I was on my way to Israel. Without a sense of belonging or acceptance by any religion, I felt like an outsider, confused and ashamed. On some level, had Avram been right?

For a few minutes, Avram let the hot potato of religion cool. But Dad, emboldened by his outburst, soon pulled out another one, this time political.

"Well, it's true you have all the elements of a good life on the kibbutz, but what about justice and equality for the Arab minority in Israel? What are you going to do about all those Palestinians who fled—or were chased—into squalid refugee camps just over the border during the War of Independence? How can you justify the creation of a state for Jews—when they've become stateless? Now they've been turned into Wandering Jews instead of us!"

Avram must have flinched. It was one thing to challenge socialist theory, but questioning Israel's right to exist was pure heresy.

"Oh, no, no, my friend, you have it all wrong! We *bought* the land from the Palestinian owners, fair and square. In fact, the American Supreme Court Justice Louis Brandeis helped raise the money. That's why we named the kibbutz after him—Ein Hashofet means "spring of the judge." And don't forget when the UN declared Israel's right to statehood, it also tried to create a state for the Palestinians. But then the surrounding Arab countries attacked us. We were outnumbered like David against Goliath, but they lost! The Palestinians fled, and Jordan took possession of what should have been Palestine. I fought in Israel's War of Independence, so I should know!"

"And bravely, too, I'm sure," Dad acknowledged, dialing back his challenge to the myth of tiny Israel surrounded by enemies, only to challenge it again. "I also fought in World War II, and I know the official version of history isn't always accurate."

"Well, of course fighting Hitler was a great *mitzvah*," retorted Avram. "But where were all the *Jewish* refugees supposed to go after the Holocaust? Don't we deserve a safe homeland where we can live in peace and dignity at long last?"

But Dad was undeterred. "You have a point, but let's admit it—the Holocaust wasn't the fault of the Palestinians."

Avram frowned like a man teaching a history lesson to the biggest doubter in his class. Dad had always encouraged me to question authority—except, of course, his own—but Avram wasn't buying this piece of critical thinking.

Naomi & Paula with Naomi & Ruth Fein on ship deck, 1949

"Look, Leon," he said wearily, "as far back as the early 1900s, Jews were already beginning to settle in Palestine. For centuries there has always been a small but continuous Jewish community in Jerusalem anyway. But after the Holocaust, we had a *duty* to bring the survivors to Israel. Don't you agree? Now we need Jews from all over the world to help build the country so we'll never face annihilation again. Let our hostile Arab neighbors figure out a solution for their Palestinian brothers. We must take care of our own."

The conversation ended in a stalemate just in time for lunch.

"Hungry?" asked Avram, clearly eager to chart a new course.

"Sure, but our conversation has been good food for thought," said Dad, trying to lighten the mood, though his pun was lost on Avram.

"Let's agree to disagree," said Avram, then added, "but in the end, you'll see I'm right. "For every problem there is a soluuuu-tion."

"Hmm," answered Dad. Now it was his turn to wonder if Avram was serious or joking.

Despite their differences, my parents and the Feins exchanged letters and small gifts over the years to come, keeping their friendship alive. So it was only natural that I write them of my plans. Thrilled, Avram wrote back that I'd be welcome to join the ulpan on Ein Hashofet, although it was already two months in progress.

But the knowledge that I'd be under the watchful eyes of the Feins only partially reassured Dad. His stubborn silence on the subject made me think he simply hoped my youthful infatuation would blow over. Although I longed for Dad's approval, I didn't want to provoke a full-on confrontation. Besides, as soon as I turned eighteen, I'd be free to make my own decisions, with or without his blessing.

In two days, Israel would rise from the sea, transforming my dreams into reality.

Chapter 6

ISRAEL AT LAST:

ARRIVING AND PARTING

O n the final night before the *Theodore Herzl* reached the Promised Land, the Mediterranean dozed quietly under a light veil of mist. But I was too excited to sleep! Determined not to miss the moment, I persuaded Naomi to stay up on deck for an all-night vigil until finally streaks of gold and apricot illuminated faint but unmistakable signs of solid land on the eastern horizon.

"Look, Crusader ramparts rising from the sea!" I stage-whispered.

"Just like the photos in the travel brochures." She yawned, annoyed to be roused.

Our seventeen-day endurance test in this rusty scow was about to end. No more stinking latrines, grinding engines, or randy sailors. But the trip had been a wonder as well. All across the Atlantic, porpoises had flashed their silver bellies in the ship's wake, and the nights had sparkled with stars. We had passed through the Straits of Gibraltar and stopped on the island of Rhodes, where we'd hiked the Monarch trail with swarms of honey-brown butterflies alighting on our hair and clinging to our clothes. The layover in the port of Piraeus had been enough time to get tipsy on red wine (there was no minimum drinking age in Greece) before visiting the ruins of the Parthenon.

Like a prisoner loath to leave the familiar security of my hellhole, a sudden fear of the unknown gripped me. The roar of the engines was now no more than a dull drone, allowing the ship to glide quietly on the softness of the sea. The vibrations that had jostled me for three weeks had also subsided to a gentle hum. Suddenly a strobe of green-and-cobalt light flashed through the mist, stippling the water in an iridescent sheen that rippled over it like quicksilver. Backlit against the sunrise, the Crusader ramparts reared up from the shore.

"That's the ancient port of Akko (Acre)," pointed out a sailor reverently as he materialized by my side. A few days earlier, we'd finally made a truce—he and his friends would call off their chase if Naomi and I agreed to help them pack up the goods they were bringing into Israel from New York. It seemed like a decent bargain. We'd even had fun ripping the sales tags from the piles of Levis so the sailors could pack them into their own duffel bags.

I wanted to savor the moment of our arrival forever—the ancient round towers rising from the mist, the sunrise making rainbows on the sea—but the sounds of stevedores and machinery soon shattered my reverie as the hull of the *Theodore Herzl* bumped up against the dock with a deep thud.

"Welcome to Haifa!" laughed the sailor, squeezing my shoulder one last time. His eyes danced, and his dark curls shone around his sweaty temples. But my eyes were not for him now. *I'm here, I'm here,* I thought. *My dream has come true!*

But the helter-skelter disembarkation into the steamy port quickly swallowed up my dreams, and after seventeen days at sea, my legs wobbled on terra firma. Suddenly several sailors thrust their duffels into my hands.

"Gingit, don't forget you promised to take these bags through customs for us," they pleaded. "Just say the jeans belong to you."

"What do you mean?" I balked, vaguely aware of something amiss.

With no time to lose, the sailors turned to a girl standing behind me and thrust their bulging bags alongside hers on the conveyor belt that led to a large shed marked Customs.

"Hey baby," they cajoled, "will you take these bags through for us, pretty please?"

"Okay." She smiled innocently.

"These jeans belong to you?" questioned one of the customs agents, his voice suspicious.

"Oh no. Those guys behind me asked me to take them through."

"Is that so?" At the shrill blast of his silver whistle, a phalanx of blue-uniformed officers surrounded the sailors before they could scatter.

"Busted!"

In the ensuing pandemonium, the remaining agents stamped our passports, waving us through to freedom and a warning: "Get out of here before those *beni zonot* get you into trouble!" It sounded like the same phrase I'd heard the passenger and the waiter use at the beginning of the trip—*ben zona*—son of a bitch, only plural. My Hebrew vocabulary was swelling already, but not with the words I expected.

Still, a wave of guilt washed over me as the police handcuffed the sailors and shoved them into their cruisers, blue lights flashing. What would happen to them? I was too naïve to grasp the gravity of the situation. The sailors' harassment had been irritating but hardly criminal in my eyes. They were just young boys, recently out of the army, having a bit of fun while doing a dirty job. Nothing in the glossy brochures I'd read about the Promised Land had prepared me for cops and contraband, and although the other girl had given them away, I somehow felt I'd betrayed them. With the romantic ramparts now behind me, the hot tarmac burned the soles of my feet through my sandals while, from above, the sun bored a hole into my head. This was hardly the arrival I'd expected.

Exhausted from our all-night vigil and the merciless heat, Naomi and I could barely keep our eyes open as we dragged our bags through the gates of the muggy port, in search of the Central Bus Station, where we'd been told to look for the bus for our respective kibbutzim.

Long before leaving California, we'd agreed to go to separate kibbutz programs in an effort to emerge from the chrysalis of twinhood. But here in this foreign land, the task felt especially daunting. Attending different *ulpanim* would be a first step on the path to separate selfhood. Although I feared the rupture of the invisible membrane that had connected us since birth, I also knew that staying together would hobble us. Like fledglings on the verge of leaving a comfortable but outgrown nest, the time had come to test our wings in solo flight.

I tried to console myself with the knowledge that Naomi's kibbutz would be only a few miles down the road from mine. But in this unfamiliar land without personal phones, that distance felt immense.

Finding the Central Bus Station at last, we bumbled our way to the *Egged* bus for Hazorea and Ein Hashofet and clambered aboard among passengers holding clucking chickens by the feet with one hand while cracking sunflower seeds with the other, leaving pyramids of shells under their seats.

"Egad, we're on *Egged*!" croaked Naomi, but I was too tired to laugh.

As the dusty bus lumbered south, I tried to take in the landscape through my drooping lids: farmers on tractors cultivated green fields dotted with fish ponds beside tidy villages of stucco homes with red-tiled roofs. By contrast, a gritty woman in a windswept black *abaya* waved her arms at some scraggly black goats on a stony patch of land beside a makeshift tent whose folds flapped in the wind like tattered black flags. Several dusty plastic water jugs sat on the ground, but not a blade of grass could be seen. I guessed the woman to be a Bedouin. Instantly, the bleak scene sealed itself into a black hole behind my eyes, and I knew I would never forget it. Was this all that remained of the woman's ancestral lands? The question rose unbidden in my mind.

The bus made an unannounced stop to pick up several hitchhikers—Uzi-toting soldiers who looked as young as I was. Road signs in Hebrew, Arabic, and oddly spelled English flashed by like frames in a movie, but I couldn't keep them in focus. Nothing felt real. *Had I landed on another planet?*

After about forty minutes, a wide, fertile valley opened up on my left. The bus pulled to a stop at a sign pointing to Kibbutz Hazorea on the right. The moment of our long-awaited parting had suddenly arrived. Naomi quickly gathered her bags. I followed her down the aisle toward the front door, feeling as if my own skin were peeling away. Brave as I'd been in initiating our trip, I hadn't bargained on losing a part of myself. Overwhelmed, I hugged her awkwardly, unsure if Naomi shared my feelings. I only knew I felt bereft without her.

As the brakes wheezed and the door hissed open, the driver peered at us strangely.

"Good luck!" I stammered. Then she was gone.

Choking back tears, I lurched back to my seat as the bus rolled on. A ghostly emptiness now filled the spot where Naomi had been sitting minutes before. The twisting road narrowed as the bus climbed the hill to Ein Hashofet. The feathery branches of dusty pine trees stroking against it comforted me vaguely. Still, the short ride felt like an eternity. Feeling sliced in half, I could hardly believe I was still alive.

When the bus drew up to the gates of Ein Hashofet, I stumbled off in a daze. Suddenly all the events leading up to this instant seemed obliterated like stars caught in the sun's glare. Despite all that had led me to this moment in this time and place—my summer job in San Francisco, the Greyhound trip across the US, Esther's wild farewell, the seventeen-day voyage on the *Theodore Herzl*, even the arrival in Haifa that morning—I felt utterly lost!

Port of Acre aka Akko

Dining Room at Kibbutz Hazorea

Chapter 7

KIBBUTZ EIN HASHOFET

My next job was to find the Feins. They were expecting me, but had no idea exactly when I'd arrive, so there was no one at the gate to meet me, and I had no idea how to find them. Heat and fatigue only increased my confusion. Passing through a large iron gate, I followed a meandering path past rows of identical stucco bungalows distinguished only by personalized front gardens.

I found myself thinking that this young country and I were almost the same age—Israel having been established by the UN just three years after I was born. Now our adventures were converging, our eyes fixed on a utopian dream of building a socialist state embodied by kibbutzim like Ein Hashofet and Hazorea. The creed of Zionism still rang with redemptive hope—the return of the Jews to their biblical land, the rise of a strong and self-sufficient people from the ashes of the Holocaust. 1963 was relatively peaceful—the previous wars in 1948 and Suez in 1956 having passed into glorified history. The Six-Day War of 1967 was a nightmare as yet undreamed with its scourge of territorial occupation, a cancer whose endless rancor would come to consume both Palestinians and Israelis. In the relative innocence of 1963, neither Israel nor I could imagine a future in which our dreams might be dashed. And so, as I stepped through the gates of Ein Hashofet, my sense of personal and political mission converged.

The nearby sounds and smells of a barnyard gave me hope of finding someone besides a sheep, chicken, or cow, but not a single worker was in sight. Had they all gone home for the day already? I stopped outside a chicken coop, hoping to get my bearings. A slight breeze blew up, but before I could welcome it, a vortex of soiled feathers anchored to bits of manure swirled up like miniature parachutes. The musty scent of animal feed and methane fumes made me sneeze and wheeze all the more. Gasping, I rushed down another path with a border of fragrant pink-and-white oleanders that soothed my senses as I discovered more stucco duplexes, lush lawns, and porches jammed with succulents, canvas chairs, kids' toys, bicycles—but still no people.

I glanced at my watch: four o'clock. As I would later learn, the afternoon hours between two and four constituted a sacred *hafsaka* or siesta, providing respite from the searing summer heat and a reward for early rising in winter throughout Israel. Still physically exhausted and emotionally raw from parting with Naomi, I too longed for a nap. Not having seen Avram and Frieda or Ruth and Naomi since I was four, I had only the black-and-white photos of that trip and my parents' stories to go on. Now I wondered what they would be like—and what they would think of me.

At last a man approached, so I mustered my courage to ask if he spoke English.

"Of course," he replied in a clear American accent. Embarrassed, I remembered too late that Ein Hashofet had been founded by American and Polish settlers.

"I'm looking for Avram and Frieda Fein," I ventured. The man smiled.

"Ah, Avram and Frieda. They were among the founders here in 1937. Follow this path and you'll find them in the third bungalow to the left of the *hadar ha'ochel.*" The hadar ha'ochel? I could barely swallow the word.

Seeing my confusion, he added, "The dining room. You can't miss it. It's the biggest and most important building on the kibbutz. Where we meet, eat, argue, hold weddings—everything."

As I followed his directions, a shiver of anticipation shot through me. I couldn't help wondering how it would feel to meet Naomi and Ruth again, now that we were no longer two sets of identical carefree playmates onboard the *Mauritania*, turning heads wherever we went.

In my head I could hear my mother retelling the tale of how we met the Feins:

> *You and Naomi were wearing bright Mexican jackets made of turquoise felt, with dancers embroidered on them in full red skirts and black sombreros. We were queuing up to board the Mauritania from New York to London. It was our first visit back to England, and you girls were only four. Suddenly, as if by magic, another pair of identical girls appeared behind us. And that's how our friendship with the Feins began—completely by chance.*

Yet thinking of my mother stirred an unexpected sadness. Just as she'd left her own mother in sailing to America, now I'd also left her. Suddenly my mother and grandmother appeared in my mind's eye like a pair of weeping ghosts, and my own tears welled up. In striking out on my own, I'd been seeking an independent path. Now I felt as if I were following in my mother's footsteps with only a slight twist in the itinerary.

Wild flowers on Kibbutz Ein Hashofet

Chapter 8

REDISCOVERING THE FEINS

When I finally found the Fein Family, they were sitting conveniently on their front porch enjoying afternoon tea. They welcomed me with open arms, yet their manner felt reserved, almost as if a phantom had suddenly materialized before them, dragging their memories headlong into the present. Frieda's gaze made me squirm, like a mother sizing me up for the teenager I'd become, and sensing trouble.

Silently softening her mother's judgment, Ruth beckoned me to a vacant chair on the porch.

"Would you like some tea?" the twins chimed in unison.

I tried jump-starting a conversation with the tale of Dad quizzing Avram about his *soluuuu-tions*. But Avram's face remained blank. Our family's cherished story didn't register so much as a blip in his memory.

Instead he shifted into the present time. "Ruth got married recently."

I tried to zoom over this chasm of time but couldn't begin to imagine my childhood playmate married at twenty-three. With their long dark braids coiled in neat matronly buns, both Ruth and Naomi looked positively ancient to me now.

The collision of past and present boggled my brain. Where were the exuberant nine-year-olds I had idolized on the *Mauritania*? Our childhoods seemed to have fled to some distant land, leaving us in the uncharted territory of adulthood. On my first day in the Promised Land, its promises diverged completely from the daydreams I'd nurtured during years of preparation.

The milky brown English tea revived me—an enduring legacy of the British Mandate in Palestine. After a moment, Frieda disappeared to rummage in the living room, returning with an armload of family albums.

"Ah, there you are," she said, as if confirming my existence. And indeed, the familiar black-and-white photo showed two sets of twins lying side by side on a ship's deck. The muscle memory of its rough wooden warmth testified to a brief, yet deeply shared experience. Yet now I realized how little we all really knew each other, then as now.

"How the world has changed," I marveled, seeing myself at age four, and the Fein sisters at nine.

"Ah," chuckled Avram, "the kibbutz has changed too since we founded it in 1937." I prepared for a when-I-was-young speech, and Avram didn't disappoint.

"When we first settled here, the members lived in tents and dug their own latrines. Our first showers were nothing more than a room with four nozzles on opposite walls—one side for the women, the other for the men—everything collective, no partitions." (Images of a naked Avram and a nubile Frieda flash unbidden through my mind.)

"Then we built *tzrifim* out of wood—just shacks really, but a big improvement over the old tents. They're used by the ulpan now, so you'll have a room in one of them."

"How about a walk to show Paula the kibbutz on her way to her room?" suggested Ruth. I was soon to discover the Spartan comfort of a wooden *tzrif* for myself—stifling on hot days, freezing in the winter rains.

I followed her along more winding paths through what looked like a large park. Firs, pines, and oleander bushes set off the modest stucco homes for kibbutz members, low-slung rows of single rooms in clusters of three or four, each with a front porch and its own patch of garden. The uncultivated land beyond remained rough and rocky. As we passed through the kibbutz, Ruth named off each area in Hebrew, urging me to try pronouncing their names. The guttural syllables lodged on my tongue and rolled like marbles in my aching brain. My first Hebrew lesson and I was not even yet in class!

"That's the hadar ha'ochel." *Ha, I've already mastered that one*, I thought, recalling my initial encounter with the man on the path who had led me to the Feins.

"And that building with the playground is a *beit yeledim*—that's where the children live and play. They don't go home to their parents at night like in the States. They sleep there too. Over here is the *machsan* (storehouse) where you'll get your work clothes. We may as well pick them up now for tomorrow."

Entering the building, Ruth pulled out khaki pants, shirts, and brown work boots from a nondescript heap. Another pile held blue work clothes. I got it. The work clothes were color coded—beige for women, blue for men.

Next to the machsan sat a steamy laundry called a *machbesa*. "You'll bring your dirty clothes here for washing at the end of the week and pick up fresh ones," instructs Ruth.

Leading me out toward the bus stop, Ruth mentioned the *refet* (barnyard), a museum, and a spring. I shuddered, dreading another flare-up of my allergies.

"The museum honors the fighters of the War of Independence, called the Palmach. That was the army before the state was established. Both men and women serve, you know. I finished last year." From schoolgirl, to soldier, from wife, to member of the kibbutz where she grew up, how predictable and settled Ruth's life now seemed in contrast to mine. Beyond the expectation of getting a good education, my life hadn't been guided by any fixed star, or so it seemed. Was that what I'd felt was missing, why I'd craved a direction, a sign, anything to tell me I was on the right path? Instead, I'd had to chart my own course. Yet ironically the Fein twins' lives now seemed utterly constrained compared to the grand adventure I felt I was embarking on. It was all so confusing. Was marriage really the endpoint of it all?

But I let these confusing thoughts go as we walked beyond a low rise, where water gushed over rocks to form a weedy pool, a small oasis in the otherwise parched October landscape. In contrast with the museum's military history, the scene felt cool and serene.

"That spring is the *Ein* in the name of our kibbutz," explained Ruth. "*Shofet* means judge. The words together mean 'well of the judge' in honor of Chief Justice Brandeis, the first Jew appointed to the US Supreme Court."

I willed my tired brain to absorb all this history. Each new word had a different taste and texture—some hard as jaw-breakers, others soft or crunchy, some hot, some clinking like ice cubes against my teeth, all of them vying to be remembered. Like a two-year-old just learning to talk, I thrilled to their sound. Though I wasn't religious, biblical poetry seemed to reverberate from the rocks and ooze from the water as I walked these ancient paths for the first time:

> *Let there be light, and there was light*
> *Let there be land, and there was land . . .*

Ruth's voice brought me back to reality. We had reached her family's porch once again.

"You'll start the ulpan at nine tomorrow and study for four hours every morning, Sunday through Friday. Saturday is the only day off. For Shabbat. The sadran avoda [the work scheduler] will also give you your work assignment tomorrow, probably in the kitchen or dining room from six to eight thirty a.m. or p.m., maybe both on some days, depending on the need."

Before I could digest all this information, Frieda rose to collect our tea cups as a clock chimed five, a signal that our somewhat awkward visit was mercifully over. I was too tired to make sense of anything—Frieda's cool welcome, the staid demeanor of the grown-up twins or, most baffling, Avram's fogginess about a story that my own family had enshrined in memory. Bereft of Naomi, I felt thoroughly unbalanced. A wave of relief overtook me when Ruth offered to show me to my room before collecting me for supper.

After seventeen days at sea, exhaustion had drained my excitement like a minus tide. My shoulders and legs shook as I hoisted my pack onto my back for the short walk to my room. I had no way to contact Naomi, but I couldn't stop wondering how she was faring. We had floated apart like continents separated into different hemispheres. My chest heaved and my cheeks burned as I pushed down the hot tears constricting my throat. Still, I was too proud and unsure of Ruth's sympathy to let her see me cry, sensing she valued stoicism over softness. But the irony of the moment impressed itself on my heart: having arrived in Israel at long last, I felt too exhausted and alone to celebrate.

Chapter 9

WORK

The following day brought another reality check. From early Sunday mornings to Friday afternoons, the ulpan work/study program would keep me running six days a week. The languid days of crossing the Atlantic and Mediterranean faded quickly as I plunged into my new schedule:

5:30 a.m.: Rise, rush to pee in the outdoor bathroom, and rinse my face in cold water
6–8:30 a.m.: Work in the dining room
9 a.m.–1 p.m.: Study Hebrew
2–4 p.m.: Rest
4–6 p.m.: Teatime
6–8:30 p.m. Evening shift in the kitchen
Friday afternoon / Shabbat: day off

Saturday was a blessed day of rest. Although the six-day workweek looked grueling at first, I soon came to enjoy its rhythm. Each day's name was also its number. Day One was *Yom Rishon*; Day Two was *Yom Sheni*, etc. with Shabbat as the peak of the seven-day cycle. Although Ein Hashofet was secular, the Jewish calendar was observed as a matter of culture. With only a single day off, I still felt more rested than after a full weekend at home where almost everything ran 24/7. Plus, every two weeks or so, I could visit Naomi in Hazorea where we'd compare notes and compete for who had learned the most Hebrew.

Soon I had settled into my morning routine. Well before five a.m., a clutch of fat gray doves chortled their raucous reveille at my windowsill. *Hoo-hu-hoo-hu-hoo, hoo-hu-hoo-hu-hoo*, they cooed, sounding more like old men clearing phlegm from their throats than gentle turtledoves. At first the birds spooked me, but as I'd soon learn, their hullabaloo could be heard throughout the entire country like a national alarm clock.

Barefoot and shivering, I pulled on my baggy kibbutz work clothes and ventured across the stony ground to the outdoor bathroom, which reminded me of camping, only with a roof over my head. But I didn't want to complain. Like the other huts for the *ulpanistim,* my *tsrif* had been built by the early *chalutzim,* who had thought them a luxury after sleeping in tents, a sacrifice Avram loved to emphasize.

The October air smelled of dust and pine pitch. With the winter rains yet to come, the dry brown needles pricked my feet. When the torrential rains began in earnest, I would have to make a mad dash, then race back to my room to lace up my clumpy boots and tame my unruly hair before joining the silent procession of shadowy figures heading toward the dining room.

At the hadar ha'ochel, I downed a mug of steaming tea and some dry toast (*tznim)* before my shift. The crew consisted mostly of kibbutz women with their hair pulled up in buns, makeup-less and uniform in their beige work clothes, and a few European girls whose ponytails, earrings, and motley clothes distinguished them from the kibbutzniks. Like me, they were international ulpan students. But a code of silence seemed to govern the early morning, and I felt shy to break it.

Tea finished, a stocky woman with a no-nonsense apron tied firmly around her ample hips and belly showed me my job: to place six sets of utilitarian white plates, mugs, knives, forks, and spoons on each of the forty tables, ensuring they all had salt, pepper, butter, sugar, and jam.

"And don't forget the *tziburiot*—one in the middle of each table," she warned, pointing to a stack of mysteriously empty stainless-steel bowls, whose use I couldn't fathom. Was this like setting out an extra wine glass for Elijah the Prophet, as we did every year at Passover, just in case he dropped in from antiquity?

By six-thirty a.m., the hadar ha'ochel was humming with shouts and conversation as kibbutzniks filled the tables I'd barely finished setting. Now the aproned woman motioned for me to push an *agala* (cart) laden with various dishes around the tables.

My brain whirled, and my hands flew as I doled out bread (*lechem*), milk (*chalav*), café, té, hard and soft-boiled eggs (*baetzim—raka or kala*), yogurt (*yauout*), tomatoes (*agvaniot*), cucumbers (*melafafonim*), porridge (*dysa*), pickled herring (*dag maluach*)—which only the Polish members seemed to relish—and something bland called *dieta*, for those with dietary restrictions. By the end of my shift, I'd learned almost the entire vocabulary of a typical Israeli breakfast.

When all but a few diners had left by eight o'clock, I still had forty tables to clear. Surveying the room, I noticed the mysterious tziburiot, no longer empty but overflowing with the detritus of breakfast: eggshells, bread crusts, soggy cereal, fruit and vegetable peelings, slimy yogurt, and spidery herringbones. So that's what they were for! I dumped the slop into a large garbage pail affixed to my cart. Then I hoisted six chairs apiece onto forty tabletops and swept the floor beneath them with a king-size push broom.

"Now comes the fun," quipped a blonde girl about my age, apparently another *ulpanista*, though we'd both been too busy all morning to exchange more than a glance. I stared at her in disbelief.

"Yes," she giggled. "Now we get to wash the floor." She uncoiled a fat hose from a cupboard in the wall, twisted the round metal handle, and directed a geyser over the stone tiles as I watched in awe. Next, she handed me a bucket of soapy water and a scrub brush with a long handle.

"Splash the soap around and start scrubbing, but be careful not to slip."

Whoosh! I tossed the contents of the bucket, and a glistening rainbow of bubbles slid out across the floor.

"Now we have to get the suds off," continued the girl, whisking the soapy water off the tiles with the suction of a rubber-bladed, long-handled squeegee called a goumy. But the process was not yet over.

"Now you get to do the rinsing," she commanded, thrusting the hose into my hands. Gripping the nozzle gingerly at first, I took aim at the far corner of the dining room and sent a surge of water to my target. A jolt of power shot through me, like breaking a taboo. Never had I imagined that flooding a floor could bring such pleasure! Whirling around, I directed the water wherever I willed it, swirling the suds toward the floor drains with a flick of my wrist.

"Not done yet," giggled the girl. "We still have to goumy off the rinse water, then wipe the wet spots and replace all the chairs." Goumy was apparently a verb as well as a noun.

My heart sank at the thought of hauling all those chairs down again, but the efficiency of the goumy in wiping away the water restored my satisfaction. Within minutes, the tiles were almost dry.

When it was finally time to devour my own full breakfast, I was ravenous! I chopped two large tomatoes, two medium-sized Persian cucumbers, and two hard-boiled brown eggs onto my plate as I'd seen the kibbutzniks do. I topped my salad with creamy yogurt, wolfed down four slices of toast and jam, tasted the stinky pickled herring, and chased it all with three cups of tea. Then I tossed my leftovers into the *tziburit*, mimicking kibbutz etiquette.

By the end of that week, my back had stopped aching, and my biceps had swelled from the daily workout of lifting two hundred and forty chairs. Along with a swifter pace, I'd picked up the vocabulary of the morning routine and mastered the art of washing a kibbutz dining room floor. Indeed, washing a floor had never been so much fun!

Chapter 10

THE ULPAN

The ulpan classroom buzzed like a Tower of Babel with students from everywhere—Iran, Australia, Sweden, England, Morocco, the US, and South Africa—chatting in their own languages when their faltering Hebrew failed them. Most were being sponsored by Ha'Shomer Ha'Tzair—the Young Guards—the Jewish youth movement of Mapam, Israel's secular political party on the far left. A few were new immigrants, sponsored by the Jewish Agency. But no one besides me had come alone, unattached to any group sponsor. Apparently the Feins had facilitated an exception for me, although the ulpan was already in progress.

Dortsia, the instructor, was an older woman with a short solid body and wiry white hair who walked with a limping gait that even the extra thick sole on her right shoe couldn't fix. I wondered if she'd been assigned to teach because her disability made physical work more difficult. Still, as a founding kibbutz member, she appeared to command fierce respect. Her welcome to me was part warmth, part warning: I would have to work hard to catch up. I promised I would, yet I worried.

Unlike me, many of the other students could rattle off whole sentences, having learned to read in Hebrew school. But I soon realized their level of literacy was an illusion—they often had no idea what the words meant, so when it came time to practice a conversation, they were tongue-tied. My problem was just the opposite: I was quick to learn by ear, but my eyes struggled over the foreign squiggles that ran across the page from right to left. I quickly rose to the top of the class in spoken Hebrew but still stumbled over reading.

The evening kitchen shift was boring but in some ways better than the hectic morning shifts in the hadar ha'ochel. Mindlessly scrubbing the gunk from giant steamers bolted to the floor on rotating steel frames gave me time to digest the events of the day. As with washing the floors, kitchen efficiency seemed to hinge on the mastery of water and drains. Once I learned that, I had the drill down. The mostly older women workers gossiped while following their well-worn routines. Absorbing their chatter, I picked up new expressions along with kibbutz news.

One evening, after I'd been at Ein Hashofet for barely a month, I tried making small talk with a woman whose English was even less proficient than my Hebrew. Despite my stumbles, her patience created a gentle rapport between us. After awhile she stepped back from the sink, as if taking my measure in the dim light.

At last she said quietly, "*At nefesh adina.*" I had no idea what this meant, but from her tone I thought it must be important, so I silently memorized the syllables in order to look them up in my Hebrew/English dictionary at the end of my shift.

Back in my *tzrif,* I leafed through the pages of my small, blue leather-bound pocket dictionary until I came upon the translation at last. To my astonishment it read like a fortune cookie: *You are a sensitive soul.* Barely believing this could be correct, I read further: *an expression usually meant as a compliment.*

I had never thought of sensitivity as a positive trait—only a negative one for which Dad had often faulted me as a child. *You're too sensitive*, he'd pronounce when I'd burst into tears at the sound of his rich tenor voice singing songs like "Little Robin Red Breast" while stroking the piano keys with his thick yet deft fingers. The lyrics about a poor bird "who died out in the cold, the cold, the cold" would set me gushing. But the disappointment in his large brown eyes would only make me sob harder.

Now I saw sensitivity in a sudden new light—more of a blessing than a curse, a strength of character instead of a flaw. If I could just learn to harness it, maybe it could serve me. At that moment, I knew I'd never forget this simple but priceless revelation from an unknown woman who had sensed something in me that I couldn't see myself. Peeling off my damp work clothes, I sank into bed in a wave of warmth more comforting than the comforter itself.

While kibbutz life would evolve beyond anything the founding fathers could have imagined, mechanical lifts for the chairs I hoisted in the hadar ha'ochel were still a dream. Likewise, the food carts I pushed had not been replaced by self-service salad bars and cash registers. Kitchens had not yet been added to individual homes, and anyway choosing to eat alone at home was still frowned upon as placing individual convenience over collective commitment. Children still slept away from their parents in their *beit yelidim*.

But the ulpan remains a living institution—a source of extra labor, potential girlfriends, boyfriends, or new members for the kibbutz. And the hadar ha'ochel still draws members together to celebrate milestones or sort out their differences in the spirit of collective community.

Chapter 11

SHABBAT

One Friday when I arrived for the last morning shift of my workweek, a tantalizing aroma of chicken soup wafted from the kitchen. *Why is Friday different from all other days?* I wondered, paraphrasing the traditional Passover question, *Why is this night different from all other nights?*

Looking puzzled by my ignorance, my supervisor patiently explained.

"We're getting ready for *Erev Shabbat*—our special Friday evening meal. By the way, all the shops in town will be closed by four o'clock and the buses will stop running too, so you'd best arrive before sundown if you're going anywhere."

"I was planning to visit my sister on Hazorea," I confided sheepishly.

"Then catch the bus by three. Of course you can always hitchhike, but you'll be the last to get a ride. Soldiers get priority over civilians on Friday so they can get home in time for Shabbat."

I raced through my morning shift, setting the tables as usual but adding plates of unfamiliar sticky brown lumps that I eyed with suspicion until I snuck a taste, while clearing up. Amazed by the delicious sugary shards that melted in my mouth—something akin to brown sugar and peanut butter spun together—I asked another ulpanista what it was.

"*Chalva!*" she smiled, wiping a few telltale bits from her own lips. "Made from mashed-up sesame seeds and honey."

Sampling a few more morsels, I surreptitiously wrapped an untouched portion in a napkin to herald a sweet Sabbath with Naomi that evening.

While my secular family had celebrated Passover and Chanukah, we had never observed Shabbat or even Yom Kippur. Fridays were simply the end of the school week, while Saturday was for sleeping in as late as possible until Mom yelled for us to get up and do our chores.

Dad ignored any organized religion on principle, a rebellion rooted in his adolescence. Crossing swords with his rabbi over the speech he was preparing for his bar mitzvah, the Jewish traditional rite of passage into manhood, Dad had stubbornly refused to make any changes. In the stalemate, his bar mitzvah had been cancelled. No wonder he had never sent his own kids to Hebrew school!

As an adult, Dad's rebellion had morphed into general alienation from institutional religion in general. But ironically, his heritage often crept into conversation, disguised in references to Jewish history, ethical codes of behavior, or the meaning of life, like a mantle he couldn't fully shake. Consequently, he'd taught me far more about the Jewish values of social justice, compassion, and critical thinking than if I'd gone to Hebrew school. Still, the weekly rituals of Erev Shabbat and Shabbat (Friday evening and Saturday) were a revelation when I first arrived in Israel.

Stolid as a stone in the bubbling brook of my enthusiasm, Dad had brooded over my aspirations for Israel in silence, but I had been too proud to beg for his approval. I could only guess at his reasons. Perhaps he worried I was simply too young.

Although he still seemed all-powerful to me at the time, did he feel his power waning in the face of my determination? But I was grappling with my own internal contradictions—fleeing from Dad's authority on one hand while trying to understand him through his Jewish roots on the other. In fact, we were becoming increasingly distant as Dad moved away from his Jewish identity, while I moved toward mine. Like two train travelers going in opposite directions on parallel tracks, we occasionally shouted at each other without hearing, as our destinies pulled us inexorably apart and our words flew away on the wind as if we didn't even share a common language. I often thought of Dad as a man of music, while I was a girl of words. Now, a poem spiraled up from that thought:

> *Dad was a man of music, but I was a girl of words*
> *He loved a staff of notes, but I loved a flight of birds*
> *He locked his heart in a room in his head*
> *I went in search of the key*
> *On foreign shores and distant lands*
> *From the desert to Galilee*
> *I gathered the mantle he dropped in the dust*
> *I mended its tattered hem*
> *Wrapping its threads over my shoulders*
> *Tunneling through history*
> *Seeking his heart through thousands of years*
> *Chasing his mystery*

Chapter 12

VISITING NAOMI ON HAZOREA

After my work shift, I rushed to my room to "make *seder*." I was familiar with the word from Seder Passover service, but in modern Hebrew it simply meant to put things in order. Another variation, *b'seder*, meant okay, as in "is everything okay?" Kibbutzniks, to my mind, seemed obsessed with order.

I shook the pine needles out of my musty braided throw rug, swept the splintered floorboards, and bundled up my dirty clothes for the *machbesa* (laundry). The ritual of making seder every Friday symbolized not only the care of my humble new home, but in a larger sense, the creation of my new world. After working for six days, I looked forward to enjoying the fruits of my labors on resting on the seventh day. It was not the literal sense of the Shabbat that thrilled me so much as its power to sustain a weekly cycle from ancient to modern times. Gathering a few things into a knapsack, I hurried to the bus stop where a few of the ulpanistim from my class were waiting to go to a party on another local kibbutz.

"I hope they have beer," laughed Lena, a gorgeous girl from Peru.

"They bloody well better," snapped a pimply English kid.

"Sorry, I don't drink," winked a guy from Iran with a dark stubble that made him look older than the others. "But I might have a little hashish I can share."

The girls giggled and rolled their eyes, but I stood apart, not knowing them well enough to party with them yet. I didn't begrudge them their fun, but they didn't seem to share my zeal for kibbutz life.

When the bus arrived, I dug out exact change, took a seat, and soon pulled the stop cord for the sign for Hazorea with all the newfound confidence of surviving an initiation. The two weeks since I'd last seen Naomi felt like eons. Disembarking, I passed through the arch of feathery pines that had swallowed her up at the entrance to her new world, and followed a path much like the ones on my own kibbutz. This time I asked for directions to the ulpan. From there I figured it would be easy enough to find someone who looked just like me. Indeed, the man I stopped gave me a quizzical look, and I realized he'd mistaken me for Naomi.

"There's another gingit just like you?"

When I finally found her, we shared a long hug that reaffirmed our connection despite our new lives. Then she took me on a tour of her kibbutz.

Hazorea looked only slightly different from Ein Hashofet. It too had a communal hadar ha'ochel overlooking a wide lawn; it too had children's houses and small stucco apartments for its members. But when we arrived at her room, I marveled at her matching desk, chair, and bed frame all made of teak wood.

"How did you rate such nice things?" I couldn't help asking, trying to hide my envy.

"Well . . . Hazorea is famous for its teak furniture factory," she explained with pride. "Can you believe these are actually seconds? It's a rich kibbutz. On top of that, most of the members receive German reparations."

"Reparations?"

"Yeah, Hazorea was founded by a bunch of German Jews—so-called *Yekkes*—most of whom came to Palestine in the early thirties, like Ein Hashofet, although some came after WWII. They were lucky to have escaped or survived the Holocaust, but many of them lost family members who stayed behind. So the German government pays the survivors reparations. By pooling their individual payments, the kibbutz has plenty of money."

As we walked to the dining room, I pondered how such unimaginable loss could become a source of abundance. But the now familiar scent of soup, steamed greens, beets, and roasted chicken soon banished these thoughts. Fresh-picked flowers and braided loaves of *challah* adorned a sea of white tablecloths. Amid smiles and laughter, the men sported dark trousers with white shirts open at the collar, while the women wore simple skirts or dresses. Well-scrubbed children darted in and out, eager to share a weekly meal with their parents.

Everyone exchanged greetings of, "*Shabbat Shalom!*"

After dinner, the tables were pushed back to make space for folk dancing. A small ensemble of flutes and drums played traditional Israeli folk songs as dancers swirled in a hypnotic circle. I watched the intricate steps with a degree of envy. When it came to dancing, I had two left feet. In any case, the fatigue from my week's work was catching up with the warm room and my full belly, causing my eyelids to droop.

Groggily I asked Naomi where I'd be sleeping, and she guided me to a room near hers, where I flopped down on the teak-framed bed and fell instantly into a deep sleep.

The next morning Naomi showed me around her work site at the *mashdela*, the tree nursery where she was learning to plant, nurture, and graft row upon row of seedlings whose names she already knew in Hebrew. Compared with my own mindless schlepping heavy chairs and hosing of floors, her job in horticulture seemed far more interesting and valuable than housework. In addition, she also seemed to know almost all the Hebrew words I had learned. How could she get so far ahead of me in so short a time? My thinly veiled envy triggered my competitive spirit, and I vowed to match her phenomenal pace.

Saturday evening, it was time to return to Ein Hashofet.

"*Shabbat Shalom,*" we called out as the bus departed. Next weekend Naomi would visit me on Ein Hashofet. The new routine would bridge our time apart and give shape to our new lives, in separate yet connected spheres.

I came to love the traditional Israeli week with its predictable cycle of beginning, ending, and sabbath renewal. Whether religious or secular, the entire Jewish population followed this rhythm, creating a sense of community I'd never before experienced. Even my single day off felt more restful than a full weekend at home. But here, with Fridays held holy by Muslims, and Sundays by Christians, three out of seven days of the week were sacred to someone, creating a certain mindfulness that was missing in the US, where everything hummed 24/7.

Chapter 13

MAKING *ALIYA*

I'd been in Israel for less than a month when the news of President Kennedy's assassination on November 22, 1963, swept through the kibbutz. At first I choked on disbelief, thinking it must be a bad joke. Without instant access to the news (television had not yet come to Israel), it was hard to verify such a horrifying act. Stunned, I ran to the Feins' bungalow to see what they might have heard on the radio. There, Avram confirmed my worst fears. I listened to the solemn announcement in Hebrew on the station of the Israeli Army radio, Galei-Tzahal, and then in English on the BBC, the most reliable news sources in Israel, each confirming the horrendous truth.

Like a bullet in my own heart, my blood drained as shock turned to despair, then alienation. How could this have happened in my own country, and to a president so revered? The mythical kingdom of Camelot, so artfully constructed by the media, lay in ruins. With the Viet Nam War and the Civil Rights Movement looming larger on the horizon, the assassination deepened my disillusionment with American politics. Dissent had always been a cherished political principle in my family. While I admired the way Dad always rooted for the underdog, his constant criticism of American misdeeds at home and abroad left me feeling powerless. Instead of joining protests against unjust causes, I longed to support causes that were just. That was a huge part of Israel's draw for me. I never questioned the myth of the tiny nation of David beating the Goliath of Arab nations arrayed against it. Here was a noble cause I could embrace.

The assassination of Kennedy made me consider staying in Israel as a real possibility. To make *aliya*—literally *one who comes up into the land*—and become an *olah hadasha*—a new immigrant—would require changing my visa status from tourist to permanent resident. Under a special agreement between Israel and the US, I could become a dual citizen. What did I have to lose?

My idea thrilled the Feins, and I glowed in their approval. Even the earnest Avram smiled warmly, perhaps hoping the seeds he'd planted in an effort to convince Dad of the virtues of kibbutz life had finally germinated. But whether or not I chose to stay on the kibbutz, making aliya carried a special status in those days (while leaving—making *yerida*—was tantamount to treason).

However, I doubted my parents would support me as enthusiastically as the Feins. Writing to ask their permission would take weeks. Slowly it dawned on me that having turned eighteen, I was legally an adult. I could make this decision without their consent. With my mind made up, I decided I would let them know only after the deed was done, at which point it would be a *fait a compli*.

The following week I took a bus to the office of the Interior Ministry in Haifa to begin aliya paperwork. But when I arrived, a line of applicants from every nation and style of dress extended halfway around the building. A cacophony of languages rose from their ranks. Daunted, I stepped back to survey the scene. Women in long dresses and headscarves stood beside others in sandals and miniskirts; men in loose turbans and dhotis squatted next to guys in Ts and stovepipe jeans. Several Orthodox men wore traditional black suits with the edges of prayer shawls (*tzitzit*) peeking over the waistbands of their trousers.

I worked my way toward the entrance to ask if this was indeed the line to apply for aliya. But a gray-bearded man in Orthodox garb blocked the door. A greasy skullcap was bobby-pinned to his wiry gray hair, and a dusting of dandruff covered the threadbare lapels of his black jacket, giving him the look of a goblin or troll.

Running his rheumy eyes over my khaki kibbutz shorts, he waived me away. "Sorry, no appointments today."

"But, sir . . . there's still room inside," I protested, pointing to some empty seats through the smudged window of the waiting room.

"No matter, *tavoi mahar,*" (come back tomorrow) he insisted, his voice rising.

I felt suddenly self-conscious of my bare legs and freckled arms. Was my outfit not modest enough for his liking? How could he bar me because of my dress? Crushed, I slunk away, vowing to catch the bus at the crack of dawn the following week.

On my next visit, I wore a long skirt and blouse with ample sleeves. But I wouldn't go so far as to cover my head with a head scarf. My secular ulpan friends would have laughed me off the kibbutz! Hoping to outsmart the wolfish little man like one of the three (non-kosher) little pigs, I arrived well before seven a.m. only to find an unruly crowd shoving and elbowing to hold their place in what passed for a line. And there at the office door sat the little man at his rickety table. But I needn't have worried. When the office finally opened, the surging crowd nearly toppled him. Taking advantage of the stampede, I barged past him too. Along with my lessons in Hebrew, I was also learning the power of *chutzpah*—the impudent assertive-ness with which Israelis gleefully challenged authority.

The chairs were quickly taken, so I shifted from one foot to the other until I was beckoned to a window at ten o'clock. I shoved my application papers under its bars and held my breath. Peering up at me, the official rose from his chair, adjusted his thick horn-rimmed glasses, and muttered something that sounded like "tea break" before disappearing into a back room as a clock struck ten.

Pandemonium broke out behind me. People shouted, shoved, and shook their fists.

"How dare you take a tea break when we've been waiting hours?"

But others were more circumspect. Some even laughed. "*Savlanut* (patience)!" crowed a man to my left, shaking his upturned palm in a gesture I'd seen before.

After what seemed like forever, the door of the inner sanctum creaked open and the man returned, casually wiping a few stray drops of tea from his beard before plopping into his seat.

"You have your American passport and the two required photos, yes?" he asked in a thick Polish accent. I pushed them dutifully under the grate.

"And are you a Jew?" he asked, as if this were a routine question.

"Of course," I answered, pointing to the box I'd checked. The form's only other choices were Christian, Muslim, or Druze, none of which seemed to apply. So I had marked the box that most closely fit my secular identity. I was not so naïve that I couldn't guess what he was getting at—whether my *mother* was Jewish—but he hadn't posed the question directly. Fearing he might prevent me from making aliya solely because I didn't comply with the Orthodox definition of a Jew, I didn't elaborate.

Along with chutzpah, I was also learning not to offer Israeli bureaucrats any more information than they requested. I'd noticed that Israelis practiced a kind of don't-ask-don't-tell code, breaking or bending the rules with the motto that it was better to ask forgiveness instead of permission.

Emboldened by this attitude, I felt indignant that my Jewish heritage should be denied just because it happened to have come through my father. After all, according to family lore, my great-grandparents on his side had taken pride in helping to found the secular reform movement in America, a tradition they had brought with them from Vienna to Seattle and later to San Francisco.

I was also learning that one of the many paradoxes of Israeli life was the disproportionate legal power of the religious minority over the secular majority, especially when it came to marriage, divorce, or citizenship. The religious/secular divide was also deeply political, pitting the Orthodox and kibbutz movement, to which Ein Hashofet and Hazorea belonged, against each other. Making aliya on secular terms, I could identify as an Israeli without religious baggage.

The tension between bumbling bureaucrats and rebellious citizens was another such irony. Many of Israel's Russian and Eastern European early settlers had learned to outfox the arbitrary rules there—only to perpetuate the byzantine bureaucracy built by the British under the Mandate in Palestine prior to 1948. Thus, the British were the only culprits everyone could agree on. Nevertheless, the habit of challenging authority remained ingrained in Israeli culture.

The sound of the official's stamp on my documents startled me from these thoughts. With a half-smile, he pushed a small square of paper imprinted with the seal of Israel through the grill.

"Congratulations, you're now an olah hadasha," he announced for all to hear, then rattled off my ID number just as loudly: 05956338. "You'll receive your official card in a few weeks."

Committing the magic numbers to memory in Hebrew, I hurried for the door. The entire process had taken hours, and now I'd have to skip lunch to catch the next bus back to Ein Hashofet in time for my evening shift. My stomach growled even as a wave of triumph rose inside me. I'd made it past the troll of a door-keeper, and the official hadn't rejected my application.

But I didn't leave quietly. The bureaucrat's announcement brought cheers from the crowd of onlookers.

"*Mazel tov, gingit,*" they yelled. "*Bharuch Ha'Shem!*" (Good luck, redhead. God be praised!)

I felt my cheeks blaze as red as my hair. A room full of nosy strangers didn't seem to care which half of me was Jewish, secular or religious, as long as I was joining their tribe. Only a huddle of Arab men in dignified robes and checkered red-and-white keffiyehs kept silent as I hurried past them on my way to the exit. Their lined faces and lowered eyes masked their thoughts, but as a *nefesh adina*, I sensed a deep resentment. Had my celebrated status as an *olah hadasha* come at the expense of their own rights? Was I a newcomer or an interloper in this ancient land?

Chapter 14

STRANGER IN A STRANGE LAND

With the approach of the weeklong Chanukah vacation in mid-December, the ulpan was abuzz with travel plans. Everyone itched for a break from the routine of kibbutz life. Eilat, a tiny outpost on the Red Sea at the southern tip of the country, was the favored destination—a full day's journey if you were lucky enough to thumb a ride. With few cars on the roads in those days, hitchhiking was the preferred mode of travel, especially for soldiers and cash-strapped students. I too was excited. This would be my first adventure beyond the confines of the kibbutz.

I assumed Naomi would come with me, but at the last minute, she reneged. Adventurous as I was, I couldn't summon the courage to hitchhike alone. Almost all the other ulpan students had already made plans, which left only Mordechai, a gawky, pimple-faced kid from New York, who was hardly my type. Swallowing my pride, I invited him along, emphasizing that we'd need to leave by seven a.m. Friday morning to beat the heat and compete with the other hitchhikers who would surely be crowding the roads.

But the next morning Mordechai was nowhere near ready as the agreed time approached. It was almost ten by the time we finally hit the road, and I was seething with irritation. The sun cut across the back of my neck like a knife. I couldn't help noticing all Mordechai's perceived flaws: his sweaty, pockmarked forehead, brushy brows, and eyes that bulged like a bullfrog's behind his thick smudged glasses; the dandruff-laced tufts of hair that poked out from the edges of his knit yarmulke, a symbol of religious observance I didn't share; and finally, the hairy heavyset legs protruding from the white socks he insisted on wearing under his heavy leather sandals. What a nerd! Already I regretted asking him along. Why didn't I have the guts to go alone? As long as I had a partner like my twin, I seemed to have plenty of courage to face the world. But flying solo felt like piloting my life with one hand tied behind my back.

"We shoulda left earlier," groused Mordechai in his nasal New York accent.

"What? You're the one who delayed us," I shot back. "I was ready by seven. I even had our lunches together."

I'd packed the traditional kibbutz fare for our *teul* (trip)—tomatoes, cucumbers, hard-boiled eggs, sardines, brown bread, apples, and *chalva*.

Mordechai wasn't going to offer much protection anyway. He'd been afraid to hitchhike, although it was common practice, with so few people able to afford a car. I'd finally persuaded him we could be safe and save money, but now he was whining again in his nasal New York accent.

"We shoulda taken the bus. What if we get kidnapped by Arabs?"

"What if they shoot at the bus?" I retorted. He flinched at the reminder of infiltrators from Jordan who had recently attacked a bus to Eilat on this very road. Luckily the driver had managed to outrun if not outgun them. He'd been hailed as a hero for his efforts. But to me, such a threat seemed remote, even vaguely exciting. Unlike most Israelis, I hadn't been raised to consider the Arabs my enemies.

Now I was stuck with this dithering dufus. Part of me wanted to blame Naomi for my predicament. She seemed to enjoy being on her own more than I did. Although she hadn't been specific, I suspected her decision to stay on Hazorea had something to do with someone she'd met. She'd hinted as much in her last note, but it would be several weeks until I could confirm my hunch. By early afternoon, my moaning travel mate and I had only made it as far as Tel Aviv—still less than halfway to Eilat.

"Stop complaining," I said for the millionth time, trying to put a positive face on our slow pace while secretly wondering if we'd make it by nightfall. Huddled in the shade of a bus shelter, we had seven other hopeful hitchhikers for competition. It was almost a social duty for drivers to pick up riders if they had room; but the real problem was how few drivers there were.

Hitchhiking also had an unwritten pecking order. First dibs went to female soldiers in combat boots and khaki miniskirts, next to their male compatriots in olive fatigues, and finally to civilians like us. Serving their compulsory two-plus years of duty right out of high school, the soldiers looked as young as I was. Yet I couldn't imagine myself clad in army togs, an Uzi rifle slung over my shoulder.

I'd never seen machine gun-toting soldiers up close. Although my father had proudly served in World War II, he and my mother strongly opposed guns on principle. Yet here in Israel I couldn't help feeling a kindred spirit with these rosy-cheeked recruits tasked with the country's defense. In those days, it never occurred to me how a Palestinian might feel on the wrong end of their firepower.

As the sun reached its zenith, the wind blew a gritty powder in my face. What if we couldn't reach Eilat by nightfall? Our haphazard plans hadn't allowed for that possibility. Finally a truck with benches in the back scooped up the last of the soldiers, leaving us a clear shot. Still I worried there might not be room for both of us, even if another car stopped. A girl alone always had a better chance of getting picked up, not because drivers had bad intentions, I'd been told, but because they assumed she needed their protection.

"Mordechai, go stand behind the bus stop," I suggested. "We'll have a better chance if the driver sees only me."

The acrid scent of the tarmac's creosote stung my nostrils, while the sun chiseled a hole in my skull and curled my hair like burning copper wire as I poked my head beyond the limited shade of the bus stop's cement shell. Wavy as a mirage, something was moving toward me from a distance. If only it would stop.

After what seemed like forever, a white pickup finally pulled up before me in a cloud of dust.

"Eilat?" I ventured.

My heart sank when the driver shook his head.

"How about Beersheba?" That would at least move us forward.

"Sure. Get in."

I thanked the driver profusely as Mordechai stumbled out of the shadows.

"Can you take my friend too?"

"No problem," smiled the man, to my relief and disappointment.

We tossed our packs into the bed of the pickup and squeezed into the cab. Stuck in the middle, my legs straddled the gearshift.

"I'm Ze'ev—the name means wolf," the man said by way of introduction. But I thought his blond hair and blue eyes made him look less than fierce. "Are you American?" Mordechai's socks and sandals were a dead giveaway.

"Yes, we're on the ulpan in Ein Hashofet," answered Mordechai for both of us.

Wanting to dissociate myself as an American tourist, I couldn't resist adding that I'd just made aliya.

"Mazel tov!" exclaimed Ze'ev. "My wife and I made aliya when we were young. I'm from Romania, and she came from India. We met during our military service, and now we have a three-year-old son."

"Congratulations!" I imagined a small brown palm in Ze'ev's large white hand.

The farther south we drove, the more barren the landscape became. Now the irrigated fields of the north gave way to cliffs and outcroppings that narrowed the desert into a V. Eilat sat at the point where the desert met the Red Sea—the same Sea of Reeds that Moses had crossed thousands of years ago in flight from the Egyptians.

As the sun dipped toward the horizon, the left side of the valley sank into shadow, while brilliant streaks of salmon and copper blazed over the cliffs on my right. By the time we reached Beersheba, darkness was fast closing in. I expected Ze'ev to drop us off somewhere soon, but instead he drove on.

"You'll never make it to Eilat this late, guys. Everyone's already home for the first night of Chanukah. Why don't you come to my house so we can celebrate together? Then you can stay overnight. My wife will be thrilled to have guests."

"Oh, we wouldn't want to impose" protested Mordechai, politely. At least he had manners. But I wasn't so sure his wife would share Ze'ev's enthusiasm for unexpected guests but Ze'ev insisted. His offer amazed me. Where else would a stranger take in a couple of hapless hitchhikers? But with nowhere else to stay, we could hardly refuse.

As Ze'ev had predicted, his wife Shoshanna greeted us like honored guests at the door to their modest apartment. The dingy exterior of their cement-block building belied the warmth inside. A Persian rug covered the floor, and a painting of the Taj Mahal hung on the living room wall. From behind the folds of Shoshanna's sari, a pale-faced boy with twinkling blue eyes and golden hair peeked out shyly.

"Come out and meet our guests, Ben," his mother coaxed. "They've come to share Chanukah with us. Baruch Ha'Shem!"

Smiling, I tried to hide my surprise. How could this child and mother belong to each other?

While Mordechai and I took turns washing up in the tiny bathroom, Shoshanna set out a tomato-cucumber salad with cottage cheese, cracked green olives, hummus, and pita. Juggling several small black skillets, she whipped up individual omelets, crusty on the outside, mouthwatering and foamy on the inside. Finally she set a pot of steaming English tea wrapped in a knitted cozy in the middle of the table. The familiar scent of home made me swoon.

"A tea cozy!" I marveled. I told Shoshanna my mother was English, and suddenly I could feel her presence as if she were sitting in the chair next to me. Whereas kibbutz tea was weak and watery, this tea had the taste of home. Unable to resist each time Shoshanna offered refills, I drank mug after mug. Had I come all this way to be reminded by an Indian woman in Israel of how much I missed my mother and her English tea?

After dinner, Ze'ev sent Ben to fetch the candelabra. "Bring the *menorah* with eight branches, the one we use only for Chanukah.

"First we say the blessing, Baruch ata Adonai, then we light the *shamash*, the candle that guards all the others; then we light the first candle with the shamas," Ze'ev explained, teaching his son, as my father had taught me and Mordechai's father had taught him, keeping the tradition alive.

Ben's eyes widened as Ze'ev guided his small hand toward the first candle and we sang together. *Baruch ata Adonai, elohenu melech Ha'Olam* . . . Blessed art though, O Lord our God, king of the universe."

"And now I get a gift!" shouted Ben, suddenly animated. Shoshanna presented him with a plush green Gila monster.

Embarrassed that I had nothing to offer, I fished out several shiny American quarters from my backpack as Chanukah *gelt* (Yiddish for money). His eyes shone as he turned the unfamiliar coins over in his small hand.

When it came time for bed, Ze'ev rolled out a pair of foam mats for us in the living room.

"Together or apart?" he asked, winking.

But Mordechai looked stricken at the mere suggestion of intimacy. To my great relief, he rolled his sleeping bag out in a far corner of the living room. Curled up in my own sleeping bag that night, my irritation with him gave way to gratitude for the hospitality of this delightful family who had welcomed me into their home like a "stranger in a strange land" on the first night of Chanukah.

Wagner Family Menorah

Chapter 15

EILAT

After a breakfast of avocado toast and tea early the next morning, Mordechai and I hugged Shoshanna and Ben goodbye before Ze'ev drove us back out to the main highway. Only the rushing wind disturbed the dawn, making lopsided shadows as I stood beside my traveling albatross. The ragged edges of a Bedouin tent fluttered in the distance, and the black-clad silhouette of a woman shooing away a few goats repeated the scene I'd noticed my first day in Israel. A sense of timelessness came over me. How many generations of Bedouins had survived this thankless environment despite invasions by countless conquerors—Assyrians, Greeks, Romans, Crusaders, Turks, Brits, and now the Israelis—over the centuries?

Suddenly the sunrise banished my thoughts in the blink of its golden eye. The desert was a land of extremes—by day a white-hot griddle; by night a blackened skillet; at dawn a copper pot; at dusk a painted gourd. Its unforgiving rocks and sharp scent reminded me of my early childhood in Texas and Kansas, where the harshness of the land had made me feel strong. I imagined the Bedouin woman felt that way too. But the gloomy Northern California coast had zapped my strength under a depressing blanket of fog, and I knew without knowing that I'd have to escape to save my sanity. I needed a hot place to dry up all my tears of self-pity. Now the merciless desert was restoring the strength I'd known as a child. I could feel my life energy surging up into my bones. Or was it the rumble of a huge semitruck grinding to a halt?

"Climb into the back," the driver shouted over the idling engine. We catapulted over the tailgate and clung to the rough wooden benches that lined the truck bed as the colossus lurched forward. A tarpaulin of canvas like a prairie schooner sheltered us from the wind and the sun, leaving an oval opening in the rear from which the road spooled out behind me like a wide-angle screenshot. Here and there, the greenhouses of an agricultural outpost broke the monotony of rock and sand, but otherwise the road wound deeper and deeper into the desert as we bumped along for hours. Just when I thought we'd reached the end of the world, the brakes hissed and the truck ground to a stop at the top of a ridge, leaving just enough time to scramble out before barreling downhill like a dust devil.

Dazzled by the sun, I could barely discern a cluster of low-lying beige buildings wedged between desert cliffs and a splash of azure in an otherwise monotone landscape. Whereas copper from Solomon's famed mines had once passed through this ancient Red Sea port, bound for Arabia and the coast of East Africa, Eilat now looked as lazy as a snoozing alley cat—one whose nap had lasted since biblical times.

But the short walk into town told a different story. Everywhere, the din and dust of construction signaled the beginnings of a modern-day port and tourist mecca. Bulldozers churned up the sandy soil; bare-chested men balancing on rickety scaffolding worked on half-finished concrete apartment blocks; the playground of a spanking-new school sported swings and a slide; while huge cranes hoisted cargo high above a new port facility. Crowds of women streamed from what looked like several factories, some in modest dresses and headscarves, others in tight-fitting halter tops and shorts, still others in billowing robes.

A brand-new city, built by and for recent immigrants, was springing up at the tip of the Red Sea where the borders of three countries met—Egypt, Jordan, and Israel. Despite the signs of development at every turn, I couldn't imagine the transformation of this dusty desert outpost into a major tourist attraction, strategic military zone, and thriving industrial hub.

"Well, we're finally here," I sighed. Mordechai gave a goofy smile.

Strolling down the only paved street in town, we soon realized we weren't the only ones on Chanukah *chofesh*. The few cafés were mobbed by other young hitchhikers like us. Parched, we ordered two fresh-squeezed grapefruit juices. Soon we were sharing our road stories with a pair of tipsy English girls I'll call Sarah and Petunia.

"Why drink juice when you can have a Maccabee?" laughed Petunia, knocking back the last of her beer. Downing my juice, I ordered a *bira levana* (light beer). Knowing the Israeli brew was only 3% alcohol, I figured it wouldn't pack much of a punch.

A few white-robed Arabs eyed us suspiciously but soon went back to smoking their hookahs. No one asked for ID. I turned to ask Mordechai if he wanted one, but he was suddenly nowhere in sight. Assuming he'd gone out back to the shack that served as a bathroom, I wasn't worried. But without him, I felt the responsibility of shepherding him on this trip slide like a heavy pack from my shoulders.

Giddy from the beer, I was more than happy to join my two new friends when Sarah announced they were going to the beach. Wherever Mordechai was, he could fend for himself. Squeezing into a makeshift changing hut, we peeled off our dust-caked clothes, stretched our bikinis over our impossibly white skin, and plunged into the cool waves of the Red Sea, shivering like jellyfish.

The salty murk stung our eyes, and without goggles we couldn't see much of the sea life below, but the swim was pure ecstasy. After drying in the hot air, we scoured the beach for coral and seashells until the cliffs around us turned ochre in the setting sun.

"We'd best get to the youth hostel right away if we want to get a room," worried Sarah.

We pulled our dusty clothes over our sticky skin and trekked back to the main street. Still no Mordechai. Maybe he'd already gone to the hostel, as we'd planned?

But once there, a beady-eyed attendant in a grimy black jacket and skullcap barred our way. He reminded me of the grizzled guard at the Ministry of the Interior in Haifa. Looking us up and down, he spat on the ground.

"You're too late. There's no room left for girls, only boys."

Embarrassment stung my already sunburned cheeks. Was barring entry to girls like me a line of work for men like him? Was there some kind of dress code at the hostel? Women in Israel seemed to wear all kinds of clothes. While some observed religious codes, plenty of others wore Western-style outfits. What to wear, when and where, was a mystery I had yet to crack in this polycultural land. Besides, was it true there was no room at the hostel for girls—or just not for girls like us? My indignation rose. Who was this man to judge us? But he wouldn't budge.

"No room for girls!" he growled again. I was too intimidated even to ask if Mordechai might have checked in.

"Oh, forget him," laughed Petunia, dragging us away. "We can sleep on the beach."

"But what about those gnats?" I protested, uneasy at the thought of sleeping among swarms of insects.

Unable to decide what to do, we ambled aimlessly for

a while until Sarah said she was starving. My stomach was growling too. Maybe we could figure out a plan over dinner. After another round of Maccabees on the terrace of the same café where we'd met, we shared orders of sizzling lamb kebabs, hummus, pita, hot peppers, olives, and the familiar tomato-cucumber salad. Yum! The simple presentation of each dish was tantalizing enough, but the taste was even more divine. I was falling in love with this food. But Petunia wasn't done yet.

"Turkish coffee, anyone?" she trilled, inviting a new batch of hitchhikers to join us.

"Where are you staying tonight?"

"Well, the youth hostel is full—at least for girls like us," she giggled.

"What about that abandoned kibbutz a few kilometers out of town?" answered one of the boys. "I hear you have to watch out for vipers, but otherwise it's got plenty of space."

I shuddered at the thought of venomous snakes. But by the time the group broke up, darkness had long since fallen, and I could no longer put off finding a place to sleep. Gnats or snakes—which was worse? I'd finally given up on Mordechai, so I was truly on my own now. Feeling an odd mix of relief, guilt, dread, and excitement, I shouldered my pack and let my feet do the walking in the direction of the abandoned kibbutz. The desert had turned suddenly very cold, and the wind whipped through my thin sweatshirt. Before long, the town's few streetlights disappeared, leaving only a shadowy half-moon as my guide.

After awhile, I made out some adobe buildings, as the boy at the café had described. The half-demolished barns and bungalows looked like an abandoned settlement all right. I switched on my flashlight, scanning for dreaded vipers. Creeping carefully around a corner, I followed the sound of something dripping and soon discovered an old shower pipe protruding from the ruined wall of a ceilingless bathroom.

Droplets glistened in the beam of my flashlight. To my amazement, water gushed out when I turned the shower handle, like Moses striking the rock! The temptation to wash away the salt and grime of the day was too much to resist, so with the moon as my only witness, I stripped naked and let the cool stream pound over me like a waterfall. Wet sand oozed up through the cracked ceramic tiles under my feet, but I didn't care as long as it wasn't a viper. Shivering but somewhat sheltered, I let the breeze dry me off. Even my dirty clothes felt cleaner after my illicit shower.

Next I had to find a sleeping spot. I crept around the side of the building and tried the handle of the first door I found. Locked. Working my way down a long corridor, I tried several more doors until at last one creaked open. But the ripe stench of snoring bodies almost made me puke. I didn't need to see a soul to know the room was full of unwashed, probably male bodies. Obviously, I wasn't the only Chanukah hitchhiker seeking sanctuary in an abandoned kibbutz. But what choice did I have? By now there was nowhere else to go and I was exhausted. Dousing my flashlight, I tiptoed over the sleepers until I found a free spot. Within minutes, I too was snoring.

I didn't see Mordechai again until we had both returned (separately) to Ein Hashofet. Through the ulpan grapevine, I learned that he'd caught a bus home that very night. Had I ditched him or had he ditched me? But neither of us wanted a confrontation, so we let the question slide. I felt vaguely guilty for how annoyed I'd been with him. But the trip had taught me a valuable lesson: I could indeed travel on my own.

Eilat in the 1950's–60's

PART II

ISRAEL—WINTER/SPRING 1964

Chapter 16

GIDON

I had just returned from Eilat when a note from Naomi appeared in my ulpan mailbox, inviting me for the next Shabbat. I was especially intrigued that she wanted me to meet someone. Without phones or internet, her only way to exchange information was by pinning a note to the message board in Hazorea's dining room with my destination on it. Anyone traveling to Ein Hashofet that day would hand deliver it like a carrier pigeon. While this system worked well, it also fed the kibbutz gossip mill. I never knew if our notes had been "prescreened." Few secrets could survive in a communal community where personal privacy was a low priority. But I didn't need gossip to guess that Naomi's *someone* was probably a boyfriend. Sure enough, when I arrived the following Friday afternoon, she introduced me to him.

Gidon was short and wiry with wavy black hair, a long nose, and crows' feet at his temples, which gave him a weathered look. But beneath the triangular hoods of his eyelids, his brown eyes twinkled. From his appearance, I guessed he was quite a bit older than we were, but I didn't want to ask.

"Shabbat shalom," I said, shaking hands.

Like most people confronted by identical twins, Gidon glanced back and forth, trying to tell us apart. It was a familiar reaction we'd seen a million times.

"Don't worry, we're quite different." We laughed in unison.

"Let me show you around the kibbutz, Paula," he offered, keen to show he knew the difference. "First let me show you the dairy where I work. It's called a *refet* in Hebrew."

"To him it's heaven, but to me it stinks like hell," added Naomi, rolling her eyes.

Picking our way past dung heaps, Gidon proudly showed off a herd of Holsteins hooked up to gleaming milking machines. *Ooga, ooga* went the machines, and *moo-moo* went the cows, their large heads plunged into feed bags. The scene made me smile, but Gidon's expression was dead serious as he described the many challenges of running a dairy: the daily monitoring of each cow's input and output; the types and cost of equipment and feed; the many uses of manure; even the intimate details of artificial insemination and how to deliver a newborn calf.

Despite the kibbutz principle that all work was of equal value, the refet obviously carried special status, which Gidon clearly enjoyed. Not only did it produce enough milk for all the members, it also supplied neighboring communities. The collective system apparently welcomed profit when it came to outside business.

Gidon seemed friendly and pleasant, and although I couldn't quite tell what he and my sister saw in each other, I liked him. He was certainly nicer than her previous boyfriend in the US, who kept finding excuses to keep her from leaving. The week before our departure, her passport had suddenly gone missing. We had turned our apartment upside down, but it was nowhere to be found. Exasperated, I blamed her for being so disorganized. After a huge fight, I made good on my threat to leave without her, riding the Greyhound alone as far as Chicago. For the first day I felt incredibly free. But by day three, I missed her so much I found a phone booth and placed a call. As if by magic, her passport had somehow reappeared, so I relented. When she arrived in Chicago, we patched things up and shared a happy visit with our grandparents.

It never occurred to us that her old boyfriend might have hidden her passport in order to keep her from leaving—only to "find" it conveniently at the last minute. What a creep! Her choice of guys had always baffled me. Now I wondered if she might be on the rebound with Gidon.

Over my next few visits to Hazorea, I would learn more about Gidon, who had already finished his three and a half years of compulsory army service and become a full-fledged kibbutz member. From that I calculated he must be about ten years older than we were. Besides his talent for tending cows, he was an accomplished folk dancer. Lithe and nimble, his feet whirled to the complicated rhythms of Israeli folk dances, the traditional entertainment on Friday nights. Naomi already knew some of the steps, but I felt too shy to join the circle of dancers.

Gidon seemed to have boundless energy, but taking a break from the dance floor one Friday night, a pensive look replaced his passion. That's when I noticed a series of numbers in blue ink on the inside of his forearm—the telltale tattoo of a Holocaust survivor.

Naomi filled me in on this dark chapter of Gidon's childhood. Born in Prague in 1935, he had spent four years in a concentration camp from age six to ten. Although he and his mother had somehow survived, by the end of the war, his father and grandparents had all been killed. Outwitting bayonet-toting guards, Gidon and the other children had learned to survive by stealing an occasional moldy potato from piles of snow. Ironically, the roles were now reversed. Although the kibbutz provided for all his needs, Gidon sometimes couldn't resist the urge to filch extra food from the communal kitchen pantry while making his own rounds as a night guard, a rotating duty shared by all the men on the kibbutz.

Classified as displaced persons at the end of WWII, Gidon and his mother had been resettled in Canada, where they learned English and set about rebuilding their lives. Gidon was finally able to attend a real school for the first time at age eleven. He had joined a Jewish youth movement in his teens and made aliya to Israel by age twenty. By the time we met, Gidon had added Hebrew to his knowledge of English and native Czech. Originally named Peter Hart, the little boy who survived the Nazis had become Gidon Lev, an Israeli citizen. I could not begin to imagine a childhood so different from my own.

Gidon

The Refet at Hazorea

Chapter 17

RENÉ

My first Christmas in Israel was a workday like any other. Only the small minority of Christian Arabs observed the holiday at all, and even then without the commercial fanfare I was used to at home. The mere mention of the holiday seemed taboo for Jewish Israelis. For them, decorated trees, twinkling lights, and heaps of gifts only served as a painful reminder of a long history of pogroms and persecution in the Diaspora.

At home we'd always celebrated both Chanukah and Christmas, so at first I thought I'd miss the twinkling tree and pile of presents underneath. But to my surprise, the utter lack of materialism with its constant pressure to buy, buy, buy brought welcome relief. *What better way to honor the Prince of Peace?* I thought. Secretly I sent a few token gifts—lightweight, flat, and unbreakable—to my family in California. Likewise, Naomi and I surreptitiously exchanged an earthen oil lamp and a soft wool shawl in a rose color as we sat beneath the symbolic boughs of evergreen she'd hung in her room. The scent brought back childhood memories of Christmas morning—the mad dash to open our gifts under the tree, strewing the living room in wrapping paper, and the ultimate letdown when the moment was over all too soon. Yet this hoopla-free Christmas with Naomi satisfied me far more in some ways. Ironically, Jesus seemed to retain more of his humanity in the land of his birth than at home, where he'd unwittingly become the patron saint of consumerism.

Since Israelis celebrated Rosh Hashanah as the Jewish new year, New Year's Eve would have been equally quiet, had the ulpan students not insisted on throwing a party. The kibbutz initially resisted the idea for fear of a drunken bash. But at last they agreed to provide some food—platters of cheese, salami, cookies, baklava, and juice—but no alcohol. I couldn't understand how they could be so politically progressive yet so socially conservative—like my own politically liberal but socially restrained parents. Undaunted, a few students took the bus into the nearby town of Yochne'am and hauled back a case of Maccabee beer for what was shaping up to be a dorm party in a *tzrif.*

By the time I mounted the front porch, the Maccabees were flowing and people were swaying to the beat of Chuck Berry belting out his Zydeco hit, "You Never Can Tell," also known as "Teenage Wedding." At home it had been one of my favorites, but here on the kibbutz, it seemed weirdly out of time and place.

I didn't have high hopes for the party, so I was hardly prepared to be swept off my feet by a cute young French guy in army fatigues. He'd only arrived on the kibbutz a week earlier, so we hadn't yet met. His tanned biceps bulged from his rolled-up sleeves, and his pant legs were tucked into his boots. I guessed he was checking on the party while on night patrol.

"Hello, shalom, bonjour!" he shouted in three languages over the din of the music. "Are you enjoying yourself?"

Was it the moonlight that threw bright streaks of silver over his dark hair? He had a sexy, devil-may-care smile and a charm that was hard to resist.

"My name's René; what's yours?" he yelled again. "You like to dance?"

Almost before I could answer, my feet started levitating and my heart expanded like a helium balloon heading straight for the stratosphere. The smoky room felt far too small to contain the emotions exploding inside me, so I dashed for the door as soon as the music ended. Like a magnet, René followed me onto the porch. Maybe night patrol could wait.

My lungs stung in the cold winter air, but my heart was aflame. Even outdoors, talking over the noise of the party was a challenge in any language, but our bodies needed no words. René's first kiss shivered on my lips like a hummingbird's wings, fanning desire from deep inside my core.

In the coming weeks, we found quieter moments to get to know each other when we weren't making out. That we didn't share a common language was not so unusual in a country of immigrants that sounded like a modern-day Tower of Babel. Compared to my fledgling Hebrew, René was fluent, but he still had a strong French accent (that was all the more romantic). Our comical mix of English, French, and Hebrew alternately accelerated my proficiency and/or confusion in all three.

Beyond the dual attractions of lust and language, I was fascinated by René's life story. With his military service coming to a welcome end after almost four years in Israel, he had persuaded his commander to send him to the ulpan ostensibly to improve his Hebrew. In reality he'd been looking for any excuse to escape the tedium of army life. When the ulpan ended, he'd have to return to Kibbutz Dan, the outpost in the far north of the country on the Syrian border where he was stationed. Although he had numerous cousins in Israel, he longed to reunite with his own large family in France, once his military stint was over.

Born in Lyon, France, on February 13, 1941, René was the fifth of seven children in a poor Jewish family. Growing up, he had shared a three-room cold water flat with two sisters, four brothers, and his hardworking parents, Haïm and Hannah. They hadn't shared a common language either, besides broken French. So our situation must have felt familiar to René.

While René seemed every inch a Frenchman to me, his nationality was more happenstance than heritage, as both his parents had immigrated to France in the early 1920s. Hannah was an Ashkenazi from Poland, while Haïm had grown up in a Sephardic community in Turkey. Whereas Hannah's first language was Yiddish, Haïm spoke Ladino, a dialect of Old Spanish still spoken by some Sephardic Jews, whose ancestors had fled the Inquisition of 1492. Like many first-generation children of immigrants, René and his siblings acted as interpreters for their parents, helping them pay their bills, make appointments, and navigate the bewildering labyrinths of French bureaucracy. But beyond their mutual need to escape from war, poverty, and anti-Semitism, Hannah and Haïm were apparently quite different in temperament and tradition.

René's family had survived World War II through a combination of luck, wit, and work as vendors at the local *marché*, Lyon's outdoor market, where they had access to the few fruits and vegetables to be found. But with so many mouths to feed on so little money, Hannah had been forced to plead for credit or barter with the other merchants for bread, milk, meat, or fish.

Running even a simple errand meant risking a gauntlet of occupying soldiers, so Hannah would wrap herself in an old woolen shawl and pretend not to understand their commands in German as she crisscrossed the cobblestone streets. Baffled, the soldiers would dismiss her as crazy but harmless. It was only after the war that she learned the fate of a brother, his wife, and their children who had stayed behind in Poland. They had all died in a concentration camp.

Through René, I learned that Lyon had played a major part in the French Resistance. When word leaked out that the Gestapo planned a roundup of Jews and suspected collaborators, the Resistance fighters would send out a warning. Then Haïm would flee to the relative safety of Grenoble, where an extended family network could offer refuge. The war had also widowed one of Haïm's sisters, leaving her to raise five daughters alone, cousins who now lived in Israel. René promised I would meet them as soon as we could arrange a trip to their kibbutz. It was these cousins who had persuaded René to follow them to Israel, where French Jews could do their military service instead of in the French Army, where they risked being sent to fight in Algeria during that country's war of independence in the early sixties.

But René's childhood hadn't been entirely bleak. He and his brothers had reveled in many escapades. They'd made a game of chasing each other over Lyon's red-tiled rooftops and through its famous underground *traboules*, the tunnels used by the Resistance fighters to strike the Germans before vanishing into their labyrinth. Like Gidon, René also loved to dance. As a teenager, he and his brothers had flocked to the popular rock and roll clubs in Lyon. René and a female partner had even placed among the finalists in a European competition. But now he had to settle for Israeli folk music.

René knew his family's war stories by heart, although fortunately he had been too young to experience most of them directly. Without even meeting them, I began to feel a huge empathy for their hardships and heartaches. Having been lucky enough to grow up in America, I'd never considered myself a product of the war that had brought my own parents together. But the indelible impact of that conflict was beginning to dawn on me. Was it survivor's guilt that drew out my compassion? Slowly I began to see how Israelis pinned their hopes for peace, prosperity, and security squarely on the shoulders of my generation of baby boomers. We were the very embodiment of renewal—of "life's longing for itself," in the words of Kahlil Gibran, the poet whose small but powerful verses I was coming to love.

One night, René sang the refrain to a popular French song:

Je t'aime, tu m'aimes, on s'aimera.
Jusqu'à la fin du monde, puisque la terre est ronde . . .

"Can you guess what it means?" he asked, then translated it into English.

I love you, you love me,
We'll love each other until the end of the world,
Just 'cause the world is round.

Was René really saying he loved me? I had no idea if what I was feeling was love or lust or a wild entanglement of both. Maybe they were inseparable at age eighteen. But he seemed so sincere. I believed him.

The market where René's family worked

Chapter 18

BECOMING A COUPLE

It wasn't long before René and I were spending most of our time together. Except for our separate work shifts, we shared meals in the hadar'ochel, drank tea on my tiny porch in the afternoons like any other kibbutz couple, and shared my cramped mattress on nights when he could get away from his bunk in the soldiers' barracks. He'd hang his Uzi behind my door before stripping out of his fatigues. Although we'd never had guns in my family, the weapon didn't bother me. It was just part of the landscape in Israel—slung casually from the hitch-hikers' shoulders, shoved under bus seats, or leaned up against the walls of museums, shops, clinics, and shrines. Since the country was still officially at war with all its Arab neighbors, I saw them through the lens of self-defense. While I would have found them threatening at home, here in Israel, they made me feel safe, strong, and proud.

With René, I felt tethered again, no longer floating as I had after separating from Naomi. His presence filled her absence and restored my sense of symmetry. I'd felt as awkward as a three-legged sack race around Naomi and Gidon while I was single.

At twenty-two, René didn't have a college degree, but I admired his accomplishments. He was an avid reader and knew the French classics. His Hebrew was still much better than mine, and he moved through Israeli society and handled money with ease. On our occasional outings to Haifa, he ordered lunch with the flair of a Frenchman accustomed to café life. The menu may have been the same simple food we ate every day on the kibbutz, but his confidence impressed me.

One afternoon, we took a short trip to Akko (Acre), the old port city just north of Haifa, to explore the thick-walled Crusader castle with dank dungeons that dated back to Ottoman times. Half hidden among the narrow cobblestone streets, a *souk* sold finely worked Bedouin rugs, leather stools, copper trays, and painted porcelain coffee sets. The curve of a small brass pot caught my eye. I watched with awe as René bargained for it.

Feigning disinterest by averting his gaze, he asked the merchant its price.

"Eight lira," replied the man, unsmiling. (Shekels were not yet the common currency.)

"Outrageous. Three lira, tops. No more," countered René.

After much haggling, they settled on five lira. The man wrapped my new/old pot in newsprint as René explained the process to me out of earshot.

"Never pay their first price. They always start high, so pretend you're not interested. Walk away, then circle back and make a reasonable offer. If you meet in the middle, you have a deal. If not, let it go. But don't start too low or you'll insult the vendor. You have to establish mutual respect before you can trust each other."

René had grown up honing his bargaining skills in the marché of Lyon, whereas my family worried over money but never openly discussed it. I admired his confidence in this department.

Market in the Old City of Acre/Akko

Emboldened, I set eyes on a set of small porcelain cups to go with the coffee pot. I could almost taste the coffee in their rosy interiors. Soon a tarnished tray with fluted edges caught my interest. It didn't look like much, but I'd polished enough of my mother's English copper to bet that a bright luster lurked beneath its gray-green sheen. After another round of negotiations, René and the vendor shook hands, and the cups and tray were ours for a ridiculously low price.

"Please sit down and share a coffee to seal our deal," insisted the merchant. Beckoning a small boy out of nowhere, he dropped a few coins into his hand. It was getting late, but it would be rude to refuse.

The boy darted away but soon returned with a gleaming brass tray. The cardamom-infused steam spiraling up from three thimblefuls of sweet black espresso made me think of Aladdin's lamp. Behind us, the sun shot its last rays over the ramparts of Akko, and a cool breeze rose from the Mediterranean, sending shivers up my spine. In the harbor below, the tide lapped gently as it had for countless eons. On the horizon, the moon rose up from the sea like an alabaster egg. Sipping the coffee, we murmured our thanks and promised to return on our next visit.

In this part of the world, personal bonds were every bit as important as the money that changed hands. Already, I treasured our shiny brass pot, tarnished tray, and demitasse porcelain cups. Each time we used them, I knew I'd remember the bearded merchant seated on his low leather stool in his white robe with its loose red cord around his ample waist, enjoying his own coffee like a sultan in his festooned shop.

Arm in arm, René and I strolled along the raised seawall as the moon shimmered over the water. Had my ancestors felt the same powerful pull of these shores too? Taking a deep breath, I allowed myself to inhabit the specialness of the moment in that place and time and feel a sense of belonging in these new surroundings, so different from anything I'd ever known.

Chapter 19

SAYING OUI

One rainy winter night, I snuggled up next to René, grateful for his warmth against a ferocious storm outside. The wool rug on the stone floor and the yellow curtains I'd hung over the cracks in the windowpanes did little to keep out the drafts. Our only source of heat was a *tanur*—a ubiquitous kerosene heater used throughout the country. To avoid suffocation, we'd doused it for the night, but its smoky residue still hung in the room's frigid air.

"Brrrr, my t-t-toes are fr-fr-ozen," I chattered.

"But our hearts are warm," bantered René. I was just sinking into sleep when his voice penetrated like an afterthought.

"*On se marie?*" he murmured.

"*Oui,*" I answered dreamily.

"Fantastic!" he cried.

The gravity of my answer bolted me from slumber. Had I really promised to marry René? My heart banged against my ribs like a wild animal desperate to escape. At eighteen I could barely imagine the next day, let alone the arc of an entire lifetime! But his proposal also made me feel wanted in a way I'd never felt before. Now that I'd given my word, how could I take it back? From an early age, I had always taken great pride in keeping my promises, whether to myself or others. Indeed, all my major life decisions sprang from my heart like thunderbolts before my head could think them through. Once I'd made a commitment, logic was powerless against my passion, so my only defense was to make a plan, however harebrained, to reach my goal.

Still, a small internal voice argued with this momentous decision. *What was I getting myself into?* While my head said *caution*, my heart whispered *destiny*. Meanwhile, my stomach churned in conflict. Hugging my knees to my chest, I locked my shivering arms over the eiderdown and turned away. Tears streaked my cheeks like the rain that coursed down the cracked windowpane. Deep inside, I knew I wasn't ready for such a huge life decision. Lost in my own storm, I couldn't find my way back from *oui* to *non*.

"Let's celebrate!" shouted René, oblivious of my reaction.

He sprang out of bed to relight the tanur. After several attempts, the sooty ring sputtered to life with a loud bang and a great belch of smoke.

"Achoo!" I sneezed. "Quick, open the door!"

But the storm's cold blast only fanned the blue flames into a cascade of orange. René kicked the tanur out the door with his bare feet, looking for all the world like a naked gnome dancing with fire. I couldn't help but laugh.

Undaunted, René shouted over the wind, "Let's make a toast!"

He poured two small glasses from a bottle of Cointreau we'd saved for special occasions.

"Quiet, you'll wake our neighbors," I shushed. There was only a thin wall between my room and the one next door.

But René was not to be restrained. He switched on the turntable and put on the record I'd bought that very afternoon in Haifa for his twenty-third birthday.

I'd agonized for hours over the choice, finally settling on Tchaikovsky's Symphony Pathétique. At least it had a name that sounded French. Having been brought up on the classics, I hadn't been able to think of anything else. But at the first strain, its melancholy minor chords and weeping violins sounded portentous. I pulled the covers over my head as if to hide from a bad omen.

"What's wrong, Cherie?" asked René, suddenly alarmed.

"Nothing," I hedged.

"But you're sad, I can tell," he insisted, reciting a poem by Verlaine to comfort me. *Il pleure dans mon coeur / Comme il pleut sur la ville.* I loved poetry in any language, and René had a knack for salvaging impending disasters with distraction.

Proud to have learned the poem in high school, I managed a wan smile, but in my ears, its meaning rang as ominously as the music: *It rains in my heart as it rains on the rooftops.*

René murmured a line from another French poet.

"*Le cœur a ses raisons que la raison ne connaît point.*"

I knew Pascal was the author, but beyond that, the meaning of his words escaped me—"the heart has reasons that Reason cannot know." Something about intuition versus reason? Was I overriding both my heart and my head?

Sensing the tension in my coiled body, René folded me in his arms and coaxed my desire until passion melted my resistance and I gave in to seduction. How could I disappoint him? Like a child playing with the building blocks of my life, I decided to let the future unfold and see where it would take me.

Chapter 20

MOVING TO KIBBUTZ DAN

B y February of 1964, the ulpan on Ein Hashofet was coming to an end, which also meant René would be returning
to his army unit on Kibbutz Dan. After my late night *oui* to
his proposal, it went without saying that I would go with him.
Still, I worried about what to tell the Feins. They already knew
René was my boyfriend, but I hadn't discussed any future plans
with them, in part because I sensed they hoped I'd stay on at
Ein Hashofet. As the time grew closer, I gathered the courage
to tell them I had some news to share.

Avram wore a serious look as he ushered me into their
small bungalow for tea the following Shabbat. He and Frieda
had once lived in a tzrif like mine, but now, as *vatikim* (senior
members), they shared a two-room apartment with a tiny
kitchen. Frieda looked up from making tea to greet me with
her usual reserve. Naomi and Ruth rose to meet me in the living
room, but their welcome seemed lukewarm. Seeing them all
together gave me the uneasy feeling of a family conference like
the ones my father would call whenever there was a family cri-
sis. As Frieda poured the tea and Ruth passed around a plate of

marbled coffee cake, we made small talk. But soon an ominous silence fell over the room until finally Avram cleared his throat.

"Vell, you haf something to tell us?" he intoned, sounding for all the world like my father, except for his Polish accent.

Anxiety mounting, I blurted out my news: Now that the ulpan was coming to an end, I'd decided to go to Kibbutz Dan with René. There, I'd said it!

In the excruciating pause that followed, the Feins exchanged agonized looks, as if none of them wanted to be the first to speak. It was Ruth who broke the silence.

"Paula, our family has been thinking about your, uh, relationship with this young Frenchman. To be perfectly honest, we're divided about it, so we'll each speak for ourselves."

Divided? I bristled. What business was this of theirs, anyway? But as I waited for her to continue, Avram cut in.

"You see, Frieda and I—well, ve vorry that you are still very young. This, uh, Frenchman, maybe he doesn't mean the best for you."

Instantly, my defenses rose like the ramparts of Akko. Why did they insist on calling him a *Frenchman* when he was an Israeli citizen just like them?

But now that the subject had been broached, Avram and Naomi launched a volley of misgivings, reinforced by Frieda's knowing nods. Their fears pierced my shield of anger like shrapnel. Only Ruth held her peace.

"As friends of your parents, we feel responsible for you ... René is too old for you ... he's taking advantage of you ... only looking out for himself ... he's lazy, sexy, and manipulative like all the French ... he's not to be trusted ... he only came to the ulpan to shirk his military duty."

As if that weren't enough, I could only imagine what they left unsaid:

*We didn't bargain on your being such a headstrong
young woman instead of the little girl we remember
from the Mauritania. We're so disappointed—we were
hoping you might stay and join our kibbutz.*

My ears burned. Entrapped, enraged, and embarrassed,
I longed for wings to fly me far, far away from this supremely
awkward afternoon with the Feins. Having enticed me to tea,
they'd treated me to a diatribe. Wordless for once, I stared at the
rug. Of all their accusations, the one about shirking his military
duty hurt the worst.

True, René had openly admitted that he'd come to the
ulpan to escape the boredom of the army. But shirking his military duty? True, he was older than I, but only by four years.
True, he was sexy—that I couldn't deny. And true, he knew his
way around the country in ways that I did not. But how dare
they cast doubt on the very attributes I admired? Nevertheless,
I wasn't about to reveal my own creeping qualms—not nearly
so much about René's character, but about my own decision to
follow him.

Only Ruth spoke up in my defense. Now she raised her head
from her hands. The room quieted as she spoke in a softer tone.

"When Naomi said we were divided, she meant we don't
all agree. That is, *I* don't agree that we should tell you what you
do. We're not your guardians, so we shouldn't interfere. I can
only wish you all the best if that's what you want to do. Dan is
a good kibbutz in a beautiful part of the country, way up north."

Soothed by Ruth's words, I fought back tears of humil-
iation. At least one of the Feins saw things differently. I took
comfort in that.

"Well," I mumbled, eager to leave, "thank you for tea, but
I've made up my mind. We're leaving next week." The excruciating hour had felt like an eternity. I couldn't escape fast enough.

All the way back to my room, I agonized over what to tell René without offending him. But his indignation quickly turned to laughter when I recounted the Feins' accusations.

"Ha, ha! Those are all just French stereotypes. Who wouldn't catch a break from the army if the opportunity presented itself? They're just too uptight to appreciate the subtleties of French *sensibilité!*"

Fearful of losing me and ignorant of my family's long relationship with the Feins, René urged me to cut my ties without looking back. Once the ulpan was over, what would I do anyway if I stayed—work full time? By René's light, Ein Hashofet would simply be exploiting my labor. Somehow he failed to mention that that's exactly what I'd be doing on Kibbutz Dan.

"You'll see, the Galilee is beautiful," he added, piquing my taste for adventure.

The chance to experience a whole new part of the country was irresistible. Plus, defying the Feins was a chance to shed the worn out "good girl" mantle I'd been saddled with since childhood. As a child, I'd always gained my parents' approval by playing Miss Responsible, but now I itched to be rid of the role.

Now René and I began planning for the move to Kibbutz Dan in earnest. He had already made a trip there to let them know I'd be coming with him and to request a room together. All that remained was to pack up our few belongings and say goodbye to Naomi and Gidon before making the four-hour trip by bus along the narrow road that wound through the hills overlooking the Sea of Galilee on its way from Haifa to the last stop at Kibbutz Dan. Although I'd miss Naomi, I felt excited at the prospect of exploring a new part of the country and experiencing a new community.

If I regretted anything, it was that the Feins, whom I had idealized as a child, had turned out to be so stuffy and meddling. But the all-powerful force of the future was pulling me forward. If gaining my freedom meant sacrificing their friendship on the altar of youthful rebellion, I could not afford to worry about unforeseen consequences. From that vantage point, I could predict how the damage to my family's friendship with the Feins would haunt me for a lifetime.

Kibbutz Paths

Chapter 21

SNORING AND SNAKES

It was still dark when I woke up at four a.m. in the room René and I were assigned on Kibbutz Dan. Swinging my bare feet onto the cool stone tiles, I scraped my toes on the rough pockmarks left by Syrian shells in the 1948 war. Badly damaged, the bungalow had long been slated for demolition but was left standing, offering a visceral reminder of bravery under fire and a temporary shelter for newcomers like us. As in Ein Hashofet, I had done my best to beautify the room by covering the worst of the shattered tiles under a colorful rug—ironically sweeping the evidence of the struggle for the land by two peoples quite literally under the carpet.

After a dash to the outdoor toilet across the path from our room, I brushed my teeth at the small sink in the bungalow's hallway. Next, I plugged in the electric kettle—tea for me, coffee for René, though he was still sacked out in bed. René was the heaviest sleeper I'd ever encountered. His snores could wake the dead. He routinely slept through the morning alarm, so I'd taken on the duty of waking him for work each morning. Although I tried my best to be patient, I felt a wave of resentment filling my chest, like a dam ready to burst.

"Wake up, wake up," I pleaded, nudging his inert form. But the snoring only intensified. For an otherwise healthy young man, it was downright scary how long he could hold his breath before gasping for air like a raspy carburetor shuddering to life. Some nights I had to shake him awake to catch a wink of sleep.

"René, *lève-toi!*" I urged again, trying the phrase in French. Still no luck.

Exasperated, I finally exploded in Hebrew. Shaking him by the shoulders, I shouted, "*Takúm k'far!*" (Get up already!) Although I'd learned the words for snoring and wake up in three languages, I couldn't get results in any of them!

"Put your feet on the floor and get up, for God's sake!"

Yanking off the covers, I tried dragging his legs off the mattress. As the covers slid away, his pale chest looked vulnerable in contrast with his deeply tanned thighs and biceps. The sight made me feel half sorry, yet half enraged.

"Grrrrr . . . ," he growled, rubbing his stubbled cheeks and yawning.

How I hated this wake-up routine! Hard as I tried, I couldn't keep from losing my patience after so many sleepless nights. Eventually my flickering resentment and exhaustion would explode into a full-blown fight. After some time, René would apologize, yet I'd still feel deeply guilty for my anger. René would then woo me with passionate lovemaking, and for a time we'd make peace—until the cycle repeated itself all over again. Yet like the pull of opposing magnets, we always found our way back to each other through physical attraction.

"Ok, ok, I'm up!" René bellowed, lurching to his feet like a disoriented sleepwalker.

"What, why . . . where am I?"

How could he not know his own whereabouts? But he seemed genuinely confused, running his hands through his tousled salt-and-pepper hair.

"I'm sorry," I softened, "but you have to get up. It's time for work."

"Ah, right, all right. Where's my coffee?" he sputtered, appearing remarkably unfazed by his rough awakening.

Vigilant lest he flop back into bed, I kept watch as he pulled on his work clothes—a brown shirt, shorts, and knee-high rubber boots, all of which would be caked in sweat and mud by the end of his day hauling irrigation pipes through the kibbutz alfalfa fields. Repositioning the pipes was a heavy and perilous job, made even harder by the slippery mud and intense heat. But another danger lurked in them as well. By night, the pipes made an ideal sleeping spot for venomous vipers. Roused from its slumber, a writhing serpent might occasionally slither out of a pipe, its massive body coiled to strike. The image terrified me, but with a safe distance between us, I secretly sympathized with the sleep-deprived snake.

Gulping down a quick breakfast of tea, coffee, and toast, we kissed each other goodbye and hurried off to our jobs in the vineyard and fields. The cool air of the still-dark morning soothed my inner turbulence. Tired as I always was, these predawn hours always felt precious. The heat of the day would arrive soon enough.

Unlike Ein Hashofet, Kibbutz Dan didn't host a work/study program, so I was now working full time. Still, I was learning new words and phrases every day, and the hands-on experience of a full-time job added to my sense of adulthood. As the most basic value of kibbutz life, work commanded the highest level of respect, even if compliments were few. A slight smile or nod of approval from my boss meant "job well done" when I wielded my clippers exactly as she showed me while thinning the vines in the spring.

Compared with my parents' highly intellectual professions in music and stagecraft, physical labor felt far more tangible. Whereas plays and concerts vanished like ephemeral dreams as soon as the curtain fell, in the vineyards, I could literally touch, taste, and smell the fruits of my labors. And although the work was backbreaking at times, it forced me out of my head and into my body. I welcomed the break from my intellectual upbringing.

Besides work, my life on Dan made me feel grown up in other ways. Like Ein Hashofet, Dan also belonged to the secular kibbutz movement that opposed the monopoly on marriage by the Orthodox religious establishment. In keeping with this principle, in the eyes of the kibbutz, living together was as good as being officially married. What I didn't fully grasp was the power of social acceptance to minimize my doubts while reinforcing my decision to marry René.

Despite the nocturnal trauma of René's snoring, my days on Kibbutz Dan took on a pleasant routine. I loved working outdoors in the *kerem*, sharing meals in the hadar ha'ochel, and exploring the Upper Galilee area on Saturdays. One of my favorite Shabbat excursions was a hike to Tel Dan where the headwaters of the River Dan bubbled up from the arid ground, creating a small oasis before flowing to the Jordan River. Tel Dan was also the archaeological site of a shrine to the Greek god Pan and the ancient Hebrew tribe of Dan. With every stone and grain of sand that lodged in my sandals, I felt eons of history rubbing between my toes.

As winter turned to spring, I was becoming more and more at ease in my new country, language, and culture. I sensed my future moving toward me with the inexorable force of a sunrise ready to burst over the horizon—a future heralding the new young woman I was becoming.

Chapter 22

SUNRISE OVER THE GOLAN

The sky was pitch black but studded with stars at four-thirty in the morning as I crept down the dimly lit paths of the kibbutz on my way to work in the kerem on the outskirts of the community. Passing by the terra-cotta bungalows, children's houses, health center, and hadar ha'ochel, my heart thumped. Being out and about before dawn felt slightly illicit—reminding me of the summer when Naomi and I had snuck out of the house at dawn to raid the abundant vegetable gardens in our Iowa City neighborhood when we were eight. Tiptoeing past our parents' bedroom, we had eased the screen door open and slipped outside. Dewy lawns sparkled in the moonlight, and the sleeping houses of our friends—so familiar by day—looked utterly transformed in the shadowy darkness. A waning moon hung in the sky. Then as now, I took a deep breath, filling my lungs with the exhilarating scent of damp grass. Every cell in my body tingled on high alert.

In the distance I could make out a few other workers converging across the lawn, the men in baggy blue overalls, the women in beige work shirts and shapeless pants. A groggy young soldier crossed my path on his way home from guard duty. Although both men and women served in the army, only men pulled night duty. Watching my fellow workers, I couldn't help noticing how traditionally jobs were divided by gender—men in the fields; women in the kitchen, laundry, and children's houses. Most teachers and nurses were female, while men held the leadership roles. I was beginning to see the gap in collective ideology between the real and the ideal. So much for a truly egalitarian society, I mused.

When I'd first arrived on Dan, I'd been assigned to work in the *machbessa* (laundry). But after several weeks of hanging out loads of sopping sheets in the hot and windy concrete courtyard, I'd gathered the courage to ask the sadran avoda for a transfer to the vineyards. At first the work scheduler had let out a loud guffaw that shook the large belly hanging over his belt.

"Are you *sure* you want to work in the *kerem* with Rivka, that crazy old woman?"

Rivka was one of the few if not the only woman to work outdoors.

As a founding kibbutz member, she was a legend but also something of a laughingstock. As a young woman in the early 1940s, she had planted the vineyards almost singlehandedly. Over twenty years later, she still tended them with fierce dedication, although their perishable fruit and short season were less profitable than the apple orchards. But as a childless wife in a society that prized motherhood, her eccentric passion aroused more jokes than pity. Despite the gossip about how hard she was to work with, I wanted to work outdoors so badly that I decided to take my chances. Working with Rivka was still more appealing than repeating the same robotic tasks with the two dour women in the laundry. So I had persisted until the work scheduler finally relented. Rivka too was skeptical at first, but once she decided to take me on, she seemed glad to teach me the tasks. For Rivka, the vineyard was a labor of love. At other times, however, she could be cranky and bitter. As her story slowly unfolded, I came to understand why. According to Rivka, the male/female roles on the kibbutz hadn't always been so traditional.

"When we founded the kibbutz in 1939, the women worked right alongside the men, digging ditches, sleeping in musty tents, building the first shelters, trying our best to prove we could work just as hard as them. Of course, we also did all the cooking and laundry too, so in reality we worked twice as hard. But once the babies started coming, ah ... that was the end of our so-called equality. The men didn't want to lower themselves to doing 'women's' work—changing dirty nappies and rocking screaming babies in the middle of the night—so they pushed us back into our traditional roles. As for me, I was only allowed to continue working in the kerem because I didn't have children. Whether that was a privilege or a punishment, I never knew."

Struggling to comprehend her Polish-accented Hebrew, I absorbed Rivka's tale in silence. Having been denied children herself, she had lavished her maternal longings on the vineyard. Yet a deep disappointment seemed to pervade even this accomplishment. The dual pain of infertility and inequality seemed entwined around Rivka's heart as tightly as the vines.

Still mulling over her story, I swung the beam of my flashlight into the shadowy eucalyptus and bushy oleanders that lined both sides of the dirt road, hoping the crunch of my work boots would ward off any snakes. Though not yet dawn, the sky was turning a shade of gray, and a few doves were already cooing hypnotically. The pungent odor of manure from a nearby *lul* (chicken coop) and refet pricked my nose. Suddenly the *cock-a-doodle doo* of a rooster pierced the predawn peace. Worry knifed through me. What if an infiltrator lurked in the shadows? (We did not yet call them terrorists.) Shivering, I quickened my pace. It was still a kilometer to the kerem situated within a stone's throw of the Syrian border.

A few signs in faded Hebrew, English, and Arabic lettering —*DANGER, EXPLOSIVES, KEEP OUT*—haphazardly posted on rusty rolls of barbed wire and broken blocks of concrete were the only visible indicators of the still-active state of war between Israel and Syria. On the other side of the barbed wire, I could hear the faint braying of donkeys and glimpse their masters as they plowed their fields. In this bucolic atmosphere, the possibility of war seemed unreal, much less the idea that Israel might one day capture and annex the Golan Heights.

One by one, the stars winked out, and a faint glow silhouetted the hills against the sky's dark dome. I knew that those hills harbored bunkers, and in those bunkers, Syrian soldiers cradled Russian-made Kalashnikovs that might well be trained on me. But the beauty of the dawn gathering over the hills eclipsed all human conflict. Part of me realized how easily the soldiers could have picked me off, but another part of me imagined they might fancy the odd sight of a young gingit girl in shorts, work boots, and a red bandana as a distraction from the tedium of war.

Light was gathering at top speed now, rimming the hills with opalescent clouds of apricot, lavender, and magenta, until finally, the sun shot over the horizon like a cannonball in a blaze of gold. There was nothing gradual or subtle about sunrise in this part of the world! The intense contrast between darkness and light made me want to cheer the new day and grieve the loss of night all at once. Despite my exhaustion at the end of each shift, I couldn't wait to creep along the dirt road to the kerem the following morning, where the sunrise promised a newborn day.

The Golan Heights later Annexed from Syria

Excellent view of Upper Galilee from bunker used to shell Israeli farmers in the 1960's

Chapter 23

THE KEREM

Temporarily blinded by the sunrise, I barely noticed the crew of other young workers gathering behind me at the gates of the kerem.

"*Boker tov*," they murmured shyly. Good morning.

"*Boker or*," I replied. "Morning light." I loved the way the Hebrew language could transform a simple greeting into a poetic call and response.

Although most of the crew were teenagers like me, our worlds were far apart. Most were from poor families whose parents had emigrated from Morocco in the early fifties. To save them from potential urban ills, the government had sent them to the kibbutz for a summer of fresh air and immersion in the socialist ethic of hard work.

Shifting from one foot to another, they awaited their work orders from Rivka. Their skeptical expressions puzzled me. Why didn't they share my Zionist zeal for the virtues of kibbutz life? Over the time we worked together, I would slowly grasp that where I sought adventure, they sensed exploitation. Where I sought acceptance, they felt like second-class citizens in their own land—poor Sephardic relatives of their better-educated Ashkenazi brethren, who dominated Israeli culture and politics in that era. What those Moroccan kids thought of my frizzy red hair and freckles, much less my eagerness to *volunteer* for hard labor under a blazing sun, I couldn't guess. Although Esther, the mentor who had inspired me to go to Israel, was far more educated than they obviously were, I was reminded of the discrimination she had described.

Since my Hebrew was still fledgling and their English wasn't much better, we communicated mostly in grunts and shy smiles as we laid out stacks of boxes at the end of each row of vines. Next we fanned out in pairs, one on each side of a vine, to snip the red and green grapes that hung in huge hands called *eshkolim*, taking care to lay them gently in the boxes for fear of bruising. When the boxes were full, we stacked them six high like leaning Towers of Pisa at the end of each row for other workers to lift onto a tractor-drawn flatbed. Teetering along the rows, it took all my strength not to topple over and send my heavy stack of boxes flying.

I was also on the lookout for chameleons that liked to hide in the vines. But they were so well camouflaged by their golden emerald skins that I could rarely see them before my fingers closed around the rough wrinkles of their soft underbellies. Staring up at me with lidless eyes swiveling in all directions, they fixed me in a prehistoric stare that took me beyond time to a place occupied only by the feel of their baggy bodies, the luscious taste of grapes, and the relentless rays of the sun.

By eight a.m. that sun was a blazing bonfire, so all picking ceased, lest the grapes spoil in the heat. Wiping the sweat from my brow, I headed for the welcome shade of the open-air packing shed at the edge of the vineyard.

My belly rumbled. Having washed down only a slice of toast with a cup of tea four hours earlier, by now I was starving. All morning, I had fantasized about cooking a delicious breakfast for the crew in the makeshift outdoor kitchen at one end of the shed. But time was of the essence. As long as I worked like lightning and didn't delay the final packing tasks, Rivka indulged my culinary efforts. As soon as breakfast was over, the trucks would need to be loaded with grapes destined for local markets. But without refrigeration, they couldn't go much farther than Tiberias on the Sea of Galilee.

Since the vineyard was too far from the main dining room to go back for breakfast, a tractor delivered the meal makings in crates and coolers. First I filled two gigantic dented kettles with water—one for Turkish coffee, the other for English tea—lit the blackened propane stove, and set them to boil. Next, I set out three types of plain unsweetened yogurt—thin, medium, and thick—alongside cracked olives, pickled fish, and piles of pita bread. Chopping furiously, I concocted a salad of fresh tomatoes, cucumbers, red onions, and bell peppers. Last, I whipped three-dozen eggs in a chipped earthenware bowl and poured the foamy mass into three large skillets, thrilling to the hiss and sizzle of liquid adhering to the hot iron edges as I swirled them into omelets. Time permitting, I sautéed onions and mushrooms and added them too.

But no matter how quickly I worked, it was never fast enough for Rivka.

"*Ya'Allah!*" she fussed, using the Arabic phrase for "Get going, by God!" But her Polish accent only made the crew snicker. With their Moroccan roots, many of them spoke Arabic, though they would have been loath to admit it lest they be seen as "Arab-lovers." Meanwhile, several of them toasted bread over the old stove, sending up black plumes of smoke from the open flame.

"Watch out, you're burning it!" screeched Rivka. More laughter. But as soon as the feast was ready, they bellied up to the packing tables to devour it.

A lined and weather-beaten woman, Rivka looked ancient

in my young eyes, though she was probably in her late fifties. When she wasn't tending the vineyards, she was defending them at Saturday night kibbutz meetings whenever a motion was made to replace them with more lucrative crops such as apples. Then she would bellow at the top of her lungs, "Over my dead body you'll tear up those vines!" Other times she'd threaten suicide or storm out of the meeting in tears, anything to save her beloved kerem. The men called her hysterical and the women rolled their eyes, but Rivka always prevailed in the end. I held my peace as she fussed over breakfast. Deep down I admired her. What she lacked in looks, she made up for in determination.

After breakfast, we finished the final packing tasks: wrapping the boxed grapes in tissue paper and loading them onto the trucks; stacking a fresh supply of empty boxes for the next day; sweeping up the shed; gathering up our tools; and finally heaving our bodies, dog-tired and dusty, onto the flatbed for the bumpy ride back to the kibbutz, dangling our legs over the sides like limp rubber hoses.

Each day after work I met René for lunch in hadar ha'ochel, along with all the other kibbutz workers, chatting and jostling over plates of boiled chicken, steamed vegetables, braised eggplant, rice, and potatoes, washed down with fresh-pressed apple juice from the kibbutz orchards. Famished as we were, the simple fare tasted delicious. In the European tradition, lunch was a full dinner, while supper was a lighter meal. I was grateful for whatever was on the menu as long as I didn't have to cook it in the steamy kitchen. Bone-weary, I could barely drag myself back to our room for a shower and siesta, the sacred afternoon break between two and four.

The whining overhead fan did little to dissipate the oppressive heat as it competed with René's snores. In fitful dreams, I journeyed back to the kerem where chameleons locked me in their unflinching gaze as if daring me to unravel the convoluted history of this land, but its paradoxes eluded me at every turn. Borders, bunkers, barbed wire, conquerors, castles, kibbutzim, and a liquid light all vied for a place in my dreamscape. Just when it was time to get up for afternoon tea, I desperately wanted to sleep until the next morning.

PART III

ENGLAND—SUMMER 1964

Chapter 24

A DETOUR TO ENGLAND

While Naomi and I were in Israel, our parents and younger siblings spent the academic year of 1963–64 in London where Dad was on sabbatical from his job in California. He cherished the chance to compose music instead of teaching it, while Mom was delighted to be near her family in England again. Jonathan, our thirteen-year-old brother, attended the International American School, and our little sister Laura started kindergarten there. The plan was for us all to reunite in California by September of 1964.

But the year had flown by, and when Naomi and I announced we weren't coming home, the shock waves rolled all the way from Israel to England! Aerogrammes flew back and forth, but when nothing could dissuade us, Dad insisted that we come to England for a face-to-face family meeting. We had little choice but to agree, and besides . . . it would be another adventure.

Sometime in July, less than a year since our first trip across the Mediterranean, Naomi and I boarded a ferry in Haifa, this time bound for Brindisi on the Adriatic coast of Italy, on the first leg of our journey to London. From there we planned to take a train through Europe, cross the English Channel on another ferry, and catch yet another train to London before hopping on the London Tube to the neighborhood of Hampstead Heath, where our parents had rented a house. Having learned the English Underground system during our year of boarding school in London five years before, that part at least would be familiar.

Gripping the ferry's rusty railing, we waved goodbye to Gidon and René until their smiles disappeared in the distance, along with the ancient ramparts and minarets of the old port of Akko. The trip took on a sense of déjà vu as a light breeze replaced the port's stale ferry fumes, gulls cawed overhead, and the ship's wake foamed in the sparkling azure of the Mediterranean. Covering 2,500 miles by land and sea, we arrived in London in one week.

On the ferry we soon met several other young people— mostly European, Australian, and South African students on a gap year—enjoying the rite of passage between high school or university before the responsibilities of adulthood set in—but no other Americans like us. But in the summer of 1964, the hordes of hippies seeking a haven from the Viet Nam War draft or simply hoping to tune in and drop out had yet to appear. Naomi and I were ahead of the curve in that respect.

Flying was still relatively expensive, so ferries and trains, popularized by travel guides like *Europe on Five Dollars a Day*, were ideal for covering long distances on short budgets. With stops in Haifa, Istanbul, Piraeus (Athens), Gibraltar, and Italian ports, ferries offered frequent service throughout the Mediterranean. Some hardy passengers even slept on the deck, despite getting soaked by sudden squalls. But Naomi and I booked a third-class cabin near the familiar roar of the engines. The horrifying peril faced by modern-day refugees fleeing political turmoil had yet to become a regular feature of Mediterranean crossings.

Although I worried about my parents' reaction to our

marriage plans, I saw the trip as a detour rather than a deterrent to my grand vision of the future. I didn't relish a confrontation with Dad, but I steeled myself against his objections. Having rationalized my own doubts by now, I was plowing full steam ahead. I wasn't about to let Dad derail a vision that went beyond Israel, to include living in France for a few years, as René wanted to do, before returning to Israel to attend the Hebrew University.

Although I could already hear Dad saying I was going off half-cocked—one of his favorite expressions—I felt I had a solid plan. I was good at making plans. Plans balanced the excitement of adventure with my need for security; plans kept my fears in check as I ventured into the unknown. Plans also reassured my parents that I was living up to their expectations as the *responsible* daughter.

My mother's opposition didn't give me as much cause for concern as Dad's. After all, she too had left her home and family in her early twenties to follow Dad to a new country. I hoped she'd understand I was simply following in her footsteps with a slight geographic variation on her model. Maybe she could convince Dad, seeing as how he'd enticed her to America, just as René was drawing me into a life in Israel and France. This was the grand logic I laid out for myself, so I tamped down the nagging turmoil in my mind and heart.

From Naomi's brooding silence, I sensed that she too had her doubts, yet neither of us dared to air them, as if to talk them over might make their shadows real. Instead, we busied ourselves with the practicalities of travel—schedules, foreign currency, luggage, and as always, fending off the advances of a few feisty sailors.

Like light passing through a veil, Naomi and I could often convey our thoughts through the slightest glance or gesture without a word. Depending on the moment or the mood, we either danced around our differences or fought them to a draw.

Like a finely tuned pendulum, our energies could gyrate wildly, but eventually we'd gravitate toward mutual accommodation. Still, we couldn't be sure of each other's thoughts and feelings without sharing them. So I was left to wonder if Naomi's internal monologues about Gidon resembled mine about René. Was she as eager to take the plunge into marriage, or did she feel forced to walk the plank?

From the port in Brindisi, we caught a train for Paris. Chugging northwest on a journey of two days and two nights, it skirted the Swiss Alps before crossing into France. The rhythmic clickity-clack of its wheels left me alternately soothed, anxious, or excited. At the cavernous Gare du Nord, we changed trains, this time heading for Calais, the point of departure on the north coast of France where yet another ferry would carry us across the English Channel.

With the vibrant midsummer colors of the Mediterranean and the terra-cotta tones of Italy and France long behind us, the color of sky and water blended into slate as we crossed the choppy channel toward the British Isles. The romantic-sounding name evoked a sudden surge of attachment for my birthplace, even though I'd grown up in the US with only a year in an English boarding school when I was fourteen, which now seemed eons ago. This wasn't my first voyage over the sea, yet suspended between continents, I felt unmoored. Where was my anchor in the world? My old insecurities wavered back at me, only to dissolve again like endless images in the watery mirror of the sea. Neither fully English, American, nor Jewish, not to mention being the double of a twin, each identity seemed to cancel out the other until I felt whole in nothing.

Luckily the fog in my brain began to lift as the chalky

Cliffs of Dover emerged on the horizon like faintly penciled outlines signaling England's southern coast. At my side, Naomi voiced the unspoken worries that had dogged us both throughout the trip.

"Too bad we wasted so much time worrying how Mom and Dad will react to our plans instead of enjoying our adventure!"

"Right! Let's definitely lighten up on the way back!" I agreed as we hoisted our heavy bags onto the train for London and sank exhausted into our seats. As soon as the porter arrived, we ordered tea. Ah! While I'd been scouring the planet in search of home, perhaps it had simply been hiding in this mug of English tea!

"Let's climb the Acropolis and ask the Oracle to predict our futures on our way home."

In two short weeks we'd be *home*—if Israel was indeed our new home. Although England would always taste of home no matter where I went, I was still intent on planting my heart in the rocky soil of Israel. Whatever else happened, my love affair with the land would endure.

Chapter 25

LONDON

The fears that had plagued me from Haifa to London evaporated as soon as my mother's smiling face greeted me at the door of the rented house in Hampstead. Dad put his bear paws around Naomi and me, pulling us into his arms as he'd done when we were little, while Laura squeezed in and Jon grinned from ear to ear. We were all delighted to be reunited as a family, as if we'd been teleported from two sides of the globe to meet at this midway point in London. Between warm hugs and ample mugs of tea, Naomi and I shared our most recent adventures of trains, ferries, and foreign lands.

The best feature of the house in Hampstead was the baby grand piano that dominated the living room, perfect for Dad's sabbatical. At the top of a winding staircase was an extra bedroom for Naomi and me. Still, the unfamiliar house didn't quite feel like my mother's family home in the north London suburb of High Barnet, where she'd grown up. Her brother Peter and his wife, Betty—my aunt and uncle—lived there now. Having spent many weekends and holidays with them during our year of boarding school, Naomi and I had come to think of the house on Manor Road as our home away from home.

All my memories and my mother's stories of London were centered in that house. When my grandparents had lived there during WWII, they had converted the upstairs into a flat which my mother and Betty shared while Dad was still stationed on a US Army base and Uncle Peter was serving in the RAF—the Royal Air Force. German buzz bombs were still blanketing London, and family legend had it that one had narrowly missed the house, sending my mother into shock. Traumatized, she had tried to cancel her engagement. As early as I could remember, that story had been a staple in the repertoire of my parents' courtship and marriage. But Dad wasn't one to accept defeat without a fight, so he'd rushed from his army base to the house on Manor Road.

"She doesn't want to see you," my grandmother had protested, trying to bar him at the door. Abandoning his usual decorum, Dad had brushed her aside and rushed upstairs to plead with my mother, as she languished in bed. "But Jeannie, you promised!" In the end, my mother had relented, forsaking her home and family for an American soldier.

Within three months of celebrating their wedding on August 16, 1944, my mother was carrying twins. The conflict that had consumed their youth and also sparked their romance continued to rage until June of 1945, barely a month before she delivered. Naomi and I would bring a happier kind of chaos into the midst of ruin.

As a child, I had found this tale supremely romantic— Dad's faith and dedication in overcoming Mom's helpless hesitation—a Yankee hero saving his reluctant English bride from death and destruction. But once the honeymoon of my homecoming was over, and my father began begging *me* to abandon my fiancé, just as he'd once beseeched my mother not to abandon *him*, I began to rethink the myth of their marriage.

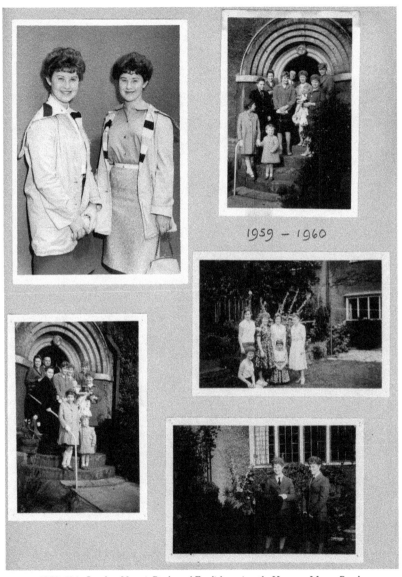

1959 – 1960

1959-60 in London: Naomi, Paula and English cousins; the House on Manor Road; Channuing School Uniforms

Jean, Jon and Laura on the Isle of Whight, 1964

Chapter 26

WEDDING DRESSES

S ewing our wedding dresses would keep us plenty busy during our visit in London. Since our early teens Naomi and I had sewn most of our clothes, so the task didn't seem too daunting. The sewing machine at the Hampstead house would be perfect for the job. In keeping with kibbutz customs, our gowns would be in a simple informal style but at least we could choose fancy material. Such fabrics were scarce in Israel, so we planned to go shopping at Selfridges, the famous department store on Oxford Street.

With a smile that was half relief and half regret, Mom wished us luck with our shopping but declined to join us.

"I need to be here when Laura gets home from school," was her excuse, but Naomi and I knew better. Our mother hated shopping. Growing up, she and her two older sisters had worn unfashionable school uniforms or matching "frocks" sewn by a tailor from the same bolt of fabric. As the youngest, she had inherited her sisters' hand-me-downs, so the color and style of her dresses rarely changed. Even on summer holidays, she wore whatever clothes would do for what she referred to as "mucking about"—sailing an old boat or going on rainy camping trips with her cousins on the Isle of Wight. Just when she might have become interested in clothes as a teenager, the war broke out so there was virtually nothing to buy. Finally, by the time she arrived in America, she had twins to dress on a tight budget and little confidence in her choices. The shopping trips of my own childhood were invariably stressful, almost always punctuated by tears of frustration. By the time I turned eleven I had vowed (another promise) to break this pattern if I had daughters of my own when I grew up.

Ironically, my mother's fashion phobia did not extend to theatre costumes; quite the contrary. With her background in drama, no effort or expense was too much where dazzle and authenticity were at stake. A wisp of lace or a length of burlap could light up her passion. I could never reconcile this paradox, much less figure out where a wedding gown might fit in. With all that in mind, I felt more relieved than disappointed that she wasn't coming with us, yet part of me regretted not being able to share this mother-daughter rite of passage.

Emerging from the Tube at Oxford Circus, the sight of the massive gray façade and gilded windows of Selfridges felt intimidating. Compared with my life on the kibbutz, the sheer *properness* of shopping in London felt overwhelming. Revolving doors soon swept us into a marbled lobby glittering with chandeliers, where a directory showed us to the fabrics department. The elevator door slid silently closed, and suddenly we saw ourselves reflected like clones multiplied by a dozen gilded mirrors. Naomi gasped. For some reason, she always felt trapped in elevators. But when our feet sank into the plush carpet of the top floor, we gasped in amazement at the magical forest of fabrics surrounding us: huge bolts arrayed by color, texture, solid, or print; plaids, florals, flannels, worsted wools; organza, voile, taffeta, velvet, corduroy, and Viyella, a soft-spun cotton that was popular at the time. A rainbow of melon, mauve, maroon, and magenta melted into olive, teal, and lavender; buttery yellows and muted champagnes competed with regal reds and royal blues. I yearned to caress their soft and silky textures until, sensing the chemical in the fabrics, my eyes and nose began itching violently. Instinctively, I reached for the tissues I always carried in case of an allergy attack.

Blowing my nose as discreetly as I could, I followed Naomi blindly to the bridal section, where she immediately fell in love with an off-white *peau de soie* fabric, whose matte finish would drape beautifully in the pattern she had chosen. We had ruled out pure white, as it did not suit our red hair and freckled skin. But the modest A-line style of her gown, sleeveless with a scooped neck, would blend in perfectly on Hazorea, where dressing up was considered bourgeois.

I coveted the same fabric for my own dress, but Naomi had found it first, and besides, we had each developed our own taste in clothes by now. We had rarely dressed alike in the past (not that this had helped in telling us apart) and wouldn't have considered starting now. Finally I settled on a slightly stiffer embossed material in pale champagne, and a pattern with a fitted bodice, wide-scoop neck, full skirt, and three-quarter-length sleeves. We were both thankful to dispense with long trains and lacy veils.

Our shopping done, we headed to the tearoom, where a prim waitress led us to a table.

"This is very *posh*," Naomi observed with a wry smile. I hoped she wasn't conjuring up some escapade designed to shock the prissy staff. But she restrained herself. "Remember the last time we were at Selfridges?"

"Of course. It was the summer before our year at Channing School right here in London. That was the most fun ever. Just you, me, and Mom tootling around England on a train, meeting all our cousins and laughing at everything, especially when people mistook us for three sisters."

Mom had taken Naomi and me to England to meet her family and get settled before our year in boarding school, leaving Dad at home in California with eight-year-old Jonathan and eighteen-month-old Laura. His music teaching salary couldn't stretch far enough for all six of us to go.

"Imagine, Mom was only thirty-seven and we were just fourteen," Naomi continued.

"Seems like a lifetime ago," I added. "And now we're getting married."

Suddenly I felt very grown up compared with the uncertain fourteen-year-old girl of five years before. Soon we were trading delicious memories of that summer in 1959 with our newfound English family like call and response.

"Tea and crumpets with Auntie Betty."

"Raspberries and clotted cream with Granny and Grandpa in their garden in the Isle of Wight."

"B&Bs with lumpy straw mattresses."

"Fried bread and stewed tomatoes for breakfast."

"Auntie Mu's Scotch pancakes."

"Teasing cousin Robert on the farm."

That memory still made us laugh. Cousin Robert, fourteen like us, had been pressed into helping with the summer harvest. Along with his sister Fiona, Naomi and I were to bring him his afternoon tea out in the fields. But we couldn't resist the chance for a prank. Instead of preparing a workman's picnic of basic brown bread sandwiches and a thermos of tea, we created a high tea of dainty triangular cucumber and Marmite sandwiches, their white crusts neatly cut off. Then we poured his tea into a baby bottle and attached a large rubber nipple used for feeding the lambs. When the queen's tea was ready, we packed it all into a basket topped with colorful ribbons. Red-faced with embarrassment in front of the older field hands, Robert had chased us over the stubbles until we fell down laughing.

That summer had been idyllic. Mom looked so young that many people took us for sisters as we traveled from London to the countryside getting to know our new English family. The three of us were enjoying every minute, until suddenly a dark cloud dampened our fun. Two weeks before the start of boarding school, an emergency telegram arrived from Dad with the shock of a fierce summer storm:

Jeannie, come home immediately. Full stop.
I can't cope without you. Full stop.
Love, Leon. Full stop.

Quick as lightning, my resentment flared. Why did Dad always seem to compete for Mom's attention? Finishing our tea at Selfridges, we compared notes. But Naomi was more understanding of Dad's predicament.

"Jonathan was probably driving him crazy, and Laura was still just a toddler."

"But he wasn't teaching summer school. Plus he had that crazy woman Mrs. Howe to cook and keep house."

"You mean the woman who held séances? No wonder Jonathan was acting up. She was also a terrible cook."

"But Mom was supposed to get us settled before boarding school. Instead we had to buy our school uniforms all by ourselves."

"But Auntie Betty did do her best to help. And we did have a great time that year once we got over our homesickness."

We went back and forth on the pros and cons of our unexpected independence that year. True, once we'd adjusted to English life, our sibling competition had diminished and our relationship had improved. Perhaps because we truly needed each other that year, we hardly fought at all.

Sipping tea at Selfridges, I suddenly longed to hop on the familiar Northern Line (colored black on the Tube's map) as

Naomi and I had done on rare weekend breaks from boarding school. Exiting the station at High Barnet, we had walked the remaining way down a steep hill to the old family home on Manor Road where our mother had grown up and her brother Peter still lived with his wife Betty. But High Barnet was too far for a visit now.

Whenever we'd had a holiday from boarding school, we had toggled between my mother's family by Tube and/or train: to Auntie B and Uncle Peter in north London; to Auntie Tre (Teresa) and Uncle Colin on an RAF base somewhere in the north; and Auntie Mu (Muriel) and Uncle Andrew on their farm in Huntingdon, not far from Cambridge. Although we were never without their support, the challenge of traveling alone in a foreign land had made us grow up fast.

Our mother had agonized over the telegram. But in the end she had dutifully packed her bags. Perhaps reassuring herself as much as us, she'd declared us grown up enough to take care of ourselves.

But Mom's departure abruptly cancelled our summer fun, leaving our spirits crushed like wildflowers after a violent storm. Although Aunt B' did her best to cheer us up, her bubbly optimism was no match for my mounting dread of boarding school.

"So that's how we found ourselves alone at Selfridges at the tender age of fourteen?" I asked, bringing the conversation full circle.

"Right. Remember how Mom insisted we order the Royal Doulton china she had her heart set on but didn't have time to buy before she left, so she instructed us to place the order?"

"Maybe the task didn't seem so daunting to her since she grew up in London."

Then as now, when it came to shopping, Mom was a no show. But having grown up in small towns across the US, taking on London alone for the first time had been both terrifying and exhilarating for us.

"I'll *never* forgive Dad for that telegram," I declared, feeling my original resentment rise again in my chest. I had felt so abandoned that it never occurred to me that my younger siblings, especially Laura, probably missed Mom as much or more than I did. The competition for attention in our family was a constant tug of war, with Mom forever in the middle.

But five years later, this shopping trip to Selfridges had been a different story. This time I had navigated the city's concrete canyons with the confidence of a young woman on a mission. Clutching our bulging shopping bags brought us both back to the challenge of the moment: Could we finish our wedding dresses in ten days?

Chapter 27

A HITCH IN PLANS

Naomi and I were busy sewing when Dad's sonorous voice floated upstairs, breaking my concentration as I fed the silky fabric into the machine's whirring jaws.

"Girls, please come down for a family meeting."

I was almost done with the seams of the skirt. The bodice and sleeves lay on the bed beside me, cut out with pinking shears like a life-sized paper doll. On the floor, shimmering scraps of material and thread transformed the nondescript rug into a magic carpet that might somehow transport me over the threshold to womanhood in my glowing wedding gown.

Naomi worked at the ironing board while I took my turn at the sewing machine. Then we'd trade places, interrupting our marathon flow only for tea and snacks. The combination of excitement and stress reminded me of high school sew-a-thons, when my girlfriends and I had turned out the latest fashions from pedal pushers to prom dresses in record time.

But Dad was insistent. Feeling rushed, I pressed harder on the electric treadle, only to watch in horror as the thread knotted in the needle and the material bunched dangerously under the presser foot. Hunched over the machine, my neck muscles tightened as I rescued the gown in the nick of time. Why hold a family meeting now? Dad never brooked any interruptions when he was composing a new piece on the piano. But the domestic arts apparently didn't carry the same weight.

The last thing I wanted now was another of Dad's paternal *talks*—more like quizzes and lectures calling into question René's limited education, his dubious ability to support us, my tender age, and my deferred college scholarship. Without raising his voice, his calm, logical tone induced unbearable guilt. Logic was a fine tool for intellectual arguments but all wrong for affairs of the heart. But Naomi's relationship with Dad was different. Where he and I butted heads, she used humor. Where I craved his approval, she feigned indifference. Despite my parents' best efforts to avoid it, I had become my mother's daughter, while Naomi seemed closer to Dad. Over time, the nicknames they had innocently pinned on us as toddlers—Pretty Polly and Naughty Nanie—had grown into lifelong roles.

But now the interruption only served to galvanize a united twin front, one that I hoped even Dad's best logic couldn't crack. Downstairs, Mom, Jonathan, and even six-year-old Laura had already gathered. I flopped down on the cushioned seat of a bow window, hoping its vaguely musty velveteen curtains wouldn't make me sneeze.

Dad (who didn't share my allergies) flared his nostrils, then slowly released the air, waiting for our rapt attention before solemnly announcing, "We've made a decision." An awkward silence and another Big Sniff followed.

"Since you girls apparently won't reconsider your, uh . . . decision to, uh, get married, uh . . . I've come to a decision." He looked as if he were trying to make the best of a bad situation without directly admitting complete defeat. Glancing at Mom for reassurance, he continued. "I mean, *we've* made a decision, isn't that right, Jeannie?"

Despite his lofty principles about equality, when it came to family matters, Dad ruled like a patriarch.

"Well, yes, *we've* come to a decision," Mom agreed, her voice more curt than encouraging.

"Yes, well, *we've* decided that since you girls don't seem ready to budge, we will come to Israel for ten days to meet these young fellows, uh, your fiancés, before going home to California at the end of my sabbatical at the end of August. Then we'll sail home from Haifa on the *Theodore Herzl*—the same horse, I mean . . . ship . . . you rode in on."

It was hard not to laugh at Dad's mixed metaphor, but I let it pass. Given his love of word play, the slip was a good indicator that his mood had lightened.

But the words he left unsaid were the ones I heard most clearly. Was he really hoping Naomi and I would come to our senses and go back to California with them? We would see about that. Still, his attempt at humor broke the tension. The image of an amphibious horse galloping over land and sea reminded me of a favorite army story Dad had told so often I knew it by heart:

Sergeant: Lookie here, we've got a new *ambidextrous* tank.
Dad: Sir, don't you mean *amphibious*?
Sergeant: Oh, no. It's *ambiguous*.

However ambiguous Dad's expectations might be, this was definitely not the lecture I had anticipated.

Suddenly we were all talking at once, but Dad had already figured out a plan. Naomi and I would leave for Israel the following week, with the rest of the family arriving in Israel two weeks later.

But by the scheming look on Naomi's face, I suspected she was cooking up an even more daring idea.

"Why don't you let Jonathan travel with us?" she asked.

Dad stroked his chin as he pondered this new twist. Having already finished the spring term at the American School in London, Jon was at loose ends for the summer. Sending him with us would give Dad a welcome break from the growing teenage tension that often erupted between them.

For his part, Jon beamed at the sudden prospect of freedom and adventure. Five years my junior, I hadn't paid him much attention as we were growing up, but now I welcomed the chance to spend some time together. With almost thirteen years between Laura and me, our age gap was even greater. By the time Laura came into our family, I had been old enough to figure out that she'd been a happy accident, conceived under a full moon on an especially fun camping trip in Santa Cruz—a beloved afterthought, more like an only child—when my mother was already thirty-five. Although I adored my little sister, we would grow up hardly knowing each other.

At last Dad turned his gaze toward Mom, his liquid brown eyes begging for her approval. Could we be entrusted to handle our unruly brother? Dad's question struck me as ironic. His doubts about our maturity apparently didn't extend to our ability to manage Jonathan on a 2,500-mile trip. Were we *grown-ups* only when it suited him?

Mom pursed her lips, as if weighing the lesser of evils— whether to let Jonathan go with us, but more importantly, struggling to accept our unexpected independence. I couldn't help wondering if she was reliving her own youthful decision to marry—a decision that had altered the course of life. At last she nodded with a sigh. If nothing else, in the short term, this new arrangement would save her from the role of referee between Jon and Dad.

Relieved of Jon, Mom, Dad, and Laura would make a pleasant traveling trio. Not only was Laura an easy child, but she and my parents shared a special bond as youngest in a long line of our family tree, going all the way back to both sets of grandparents, all of whom were also the youngest of their siblings. I vaguely envied their exclusive membership in the Club of Youngests. As a firstborn by only fifteen minutes, my honor was mixed: expected to shoulder more responsibility on one hand but challenged by Naomi on the other.

"How about a cup of tea?" Mom offered, sealing the new travel plans which had lightened the energy in the room like a fresh breeze, sweeping away my negative thoughts.

The following week whirred by as Naomi and I feverishly finished our dresses. Various aunts, uncles, and cousins must have appeared and vanished in a blur as we bought tickets, packed bags, and pored over maps. All the while, Jonathan wore a continuously crinkly grin at the prospect of visiting the Acropolis, a dream come true for a boy whose favorite subject was ancient history. Now he would get to see the dusty ruins he knew only from books.

Chapter 28

JONATHAN COMES TO ISRAEL

Even with the added responsibility of shepherding Jonathan back to Israel, I felt giddy with independence as the weight of Dad's control slipped away. Having already made the one-way trip unscathed, perhaps our parents' confidence hadn't been misplaced. Now, traveling in reverse, the journey felt strangely familiar yet also new as we caught a train from London to the south coast, crossed the English Channel by ferry (no Chunnel then), rode the Eurorail through France and northern Italy, and back to Brindisi on the Italian coast to catch a final ferry for Haifa with a stop in Athens.

Throughout the trip, Jonathan's eyes twinkled with growing excitement. His only complaint was hunger. With the voracious appetite of a teenager, he was constantly famished. After several days of frugal snacking on the train through France, he was clamoring for a real meal, so we took advantage of a half-day layover in Italy. Sitting under a tricolored umbrella at an outdoor bistro, Jon wolfed down a huge plate of spaghetti and meatballs and polished off an entire loaf of crusty bread slathered with butter. But I soon regretted ordering a bottle of

Chianti (there seemed to be no age limit on alcohol) when Jon's tongue began wagging and his cheeks turned rosy.

"*Basta*," I said finally, setting bottle out of his reach.

Arriving in Greece, Jon couldn't wait to visit the Acropolis and the Parthenon. He knew all the Athenian gods and goddesses by name (as well as the Romans and Egyptians) as if they were old friends.

"I finally get to meet Athena and Zeus!" he shouted, racing up the rocky paths to pay homage to his idols, his face as red as his hair in the blazing summer heat.

Two nights and a day later, our ship docked in Haifa. As planned, Gidon and René were waiting for us at the port.

"Meet Jonathan," we chimed.

"Ah, *Yo-na-tan*," roared René, enunciating each syllable of Jon's name in Hebrew. "Do you know what your name means?"

Baffled, Jon took a step back. Who was this strange man with a heavy French accent, and why was he asking such an intimate question? But René persevered with the zeal of a prophet initiating an acolyte into the tribe.

"Well, I'll tell you. *Yo* means God, and *natan* means given. So *Yo-na-tan* means God-given or gift of God! Now you know you have a very special name!"

Jon only looked more confused as he squinted into the sun and shifted on one leg, trying to get his bearings in these strange new surroundings. But the significance of the moment was not lost on me. Even if my parents had known the meaning of his name when they chose it, by now they hardly thought of Jonathan as heaven sent—quite the opposite. Although he excelled in school, Jon rarely lived up to Dad's expectations of perfection at home. Unlike Dad, Jon was not especially competitive in athletics, and Dad would become frustrated and critical. Worse, at age eight, Jon still wasn't dry at night. Dad seemed to take this as a moral failing. I remembered my father's angry voice rousing him from his sodden bed and calling him a Wetster as he hauled Jon into a cold bath. (Enuresis wasn't well understood in those days.) Their hostility had only grown as Jon reached adolescence, with Mom assuming the role of mediator, her loyalties torn between husband and son. For all these reasons, it was hard to imagine my parents considering Jon a gift of God. But now was not the time to dampen the joy of our arrival.

As the sun arched higher over the steamy port, the time came to go our separate ways. Naomi and I had worked well enough together over the past several weeks—perhaps needing solidarity to face our parents—but the pressure of coordinating every move in close quarters for that long had worn our patience thin. We were more than ready for some individual space. Our plan was for Jonathan to accompany René and me to Kibbutz Dan for the first week, then for him to spend the next with Naomi and Gidon on Hazorea. Then we would all meet up when our parents and Laura arrived.

After a quick lunch at a falafel stand, we headed for the Central Bus Station, where Naomi and Gidon took the short ride to Hazorea, while René, Jon, and I boarded a bus for the four-hour trip to Kibbutz Dan. Bumping over the potholed road, Jon marveled at the Crusader castles, Bedouin tents, and the sparkling Sea of Galilee, mesmerized by the site of so much history strewn among the rocks and ruins.

Venus was still glowing on the dark horizon when I roused Jon well before dawn the next day.

"Rise and shine—time for work," I chirped. "And don't forget your hat. It's going to be hot in the vineyards as soon as the sun comes up."

He roused himself from a sound sleep in the vacant room next to ours that I'd fixed up as best I could. The war-ravaged walls had been hard to hide, but I had passed off the pocked plaster as living evidence of history. Jon was impressed.

The summer harvest was in full swing, and I knew Rivka would be glad to have an extra pair of hands, if only for a week. After a quick cup of tea and a few bites of toast, I led Jon along the shadowy path to the vineyards, assuring him he'd get a full breakfast later.

"See those hills over there? That's Syria," I said, gesturing toward the Golan Heights as the sun rose in a blaze of gold and magenta.

"Are machine guns trained on us up there like you said?" Jon asked with a mix of fear and excitement, wanting to verify the stories I'd told him on our trip.

"Yes, maybe, but the soldiers are probably just bored because we're in a peaceful period now, so don't worry." I didn't want to alarm him. As if on cue, the Syrian donkeys began braying in the nearby fields.

"You could do worse than donkeys for enemies," laughed Jon, relieved.

As we began picking the grapes, row by rows, I demonstrated the proper way to lift up the leaves and carefully cull the fullest bunches underneath.

"Cradle them in your hands so they won't fall when you cut the stem with your clippers, then lay them gently in the boxes. When the box is full, carry it to the end of the row and stack it carefully so it won't topple over."

Jon worked diligently on one side of the vine while I

supervised from the other. After awhile, he progressed on his own, lifting the leaves and gasping at the huge hands of grapes underneath.

"Look at this gigantic bunch!" He beamed, wiping the juice of a stray grape from his chin.

"You look like Adam in the Garden of Eden," I laughed. "Only with grapes instead of an apple."

"Yeah, an Adam's apple," Jon joked, popping another purple grape into his mouth.

His innocent joy touched my heart, and I knew I'd remember the moment forever.

By eight a.m. the sun was too hot to pick the grapes without damaging them (never mind the chance of heatstroke for the crew), so we loaded the stacked boxes onto flatbeds and traipsed to the packing shed. Our work boots left powdery prints in the dusty road. The grapes would stay cool enough in the shade of the shed to allow for a breakfast break before loading them onto trucks for the local market.

"I'm starved!" moaned Jon.

"First we have to *make* it." Explaining that the kerem was too far from the main dining room, I showed him the breakfast makings that the kitchen had sent out by tractor. As I knew he would, Jon beamed at the sight of the brown eggs, pita, hummus, tomatoes, cucumbers, red onions, bell peppers, black and green olives, yogurt, coffee, tea, and juice awaiting him.

"Hey, don't just stand there," I teased, tossing a damp cloth in his direction. "Wipe down the tables, and set out the olives, yogurt, salt, and pepper." Jon complied without complaint. I'd never seen him so obedient at home.

Jon watched wide-eyed as I set the dented kettles to boil, chopped up the vegetables, beat the eggs, and grated the cheese for the omelets. By now I was a pro at controlling the unpredictable flames of the blackened propane range.

Still, Rivka couldn't resist hurrying me with her usual

"*Maher-maher!*" (Hurry up.) Her arthritic limp seemed worse, but I'd learned to ignore her crotchety scolding. Soon we all sat down to relish our hard-earned breakfast.

"This Israeli breakfast sure beats cornflakes," Jon said, practically inhaling his plate before going back for a second helping.

For the next six days we repeated the harvest ritual—trudging out to the vineyards before dawn to pick and pack the glistening grapes until our stomachs growled for breakfast. Exhausted, we welcomed Saturday with a gratitude bordering on ecstasy. We didn't need a synagogue to worship our single day of rest.

"Let's take Jon to the headwaters of the Dan," I suggested when we were all rested. It was one of my favorite hikes, short enough not to be exhausting in the lingering heat of a late afternoon, yet full of surprises. Following a rocky path beyond the kibbutz toward a clump of trees, we came upon a spot where water suddenly bubbled up. Where the earth had been brown and parched only moments before, a carpet of emerald water lilies and tiny purple flowers now undulated in the filtered sunlight of a feathery canopy. Stunned, Jon stopped in his tracks, as breathless as I too had been at first sight.

"Wow, it's magical!" He gasped.

"What's more, the River Jordan begins at this very spot."

"You mean this little spring carries that much ancient history?"

We stood in silence, absorbing the water's burbling sound, so simple yet profound, each of us pondering the significance of our own small presence in the long chain of history that had led us to this site.

After a few minutes, Jon began humming, "River Jordan is muddy and wide, milk and honey on the other side—hallelooo-ooo-ooo-ya!" Shadows and light played over his trademark grin.

Yo-na-tan, I thought. God's gift, shadows and light. That was my brother. In that moment, he looked as happy as I would ever know him. I would cherish his boyish joy in discovering a huge hand of grapes hidden on a vine or the soft body of a chameleon under his palm when, years later, he joined the march of history he loved so well.

Jonathan in his teens

Chapter 29

HOPES AND FEARS

My regular trips to the port of Haifa were becoming a rite of passage. The guard must have noticed it too as I opened my bag for inspection at its massive iron gates.

"Whoa, Gingit, weren't you here just a couple of weeks ago?" Seeing Naomi too, he did a double take. "Another gingit? What are you, *te'umot* [twins]?"

"Oh no, we're not even related," Naomi deadpanned. Dumbfounded, the young soldier stared even harder before realizing the joke was on him.

Like other soldiers, he looked barely older than we were.

"So, where are you off to now?"

Before we could answer, René gave him the full megillah of our story. "They're here to greet their parents who are coming to meet us—me and this guy over there"—he motioned to Gidon—"before we get married. It's a special day, don't you agree?"

"Mazel tov!" shouted the soldier, clapping René and Gidon on the back like old friends. "May the parents fall in love with Israel just like you've fallen for their daughters! God willing, they'll settle here too so they can be close to their grandchildren."

His simple assumption that my family would (or should) naturally want to join the great Jewish ingathering belied the complexities of the situation. But the personal banter broke the tension between excitement and fear as we hurried toward the dock, his last bit of advice echoing in my ears.

"Hey gingit, get married soon or you'll end up in the army guarding this stinking gate all day like me!"

I couldn't imagine myself in his position, but there was a serious side to his silly warning. Only single women had to serve in the IDF. By getting married, was I avoiding military duty? But now was not the time for such worries. With three low blasts, the ferry pulled into view. I strained for a glimpse of my family's trademark freckles and red hair (except for Mom's, which she called dishwater brown) among the mostly dark complexions of the other passengers.

"There they are!" shouted Naomi, pointing suddenly at the crowd.

Squinting into the sun, all I could see were black dots.

"Up there, on the gangplank. See Laura's pigtails swinging in the breeze? Mom and Dad are right behind."

Zeroing in, I caught sight of a pair of red-gold braids swaying side to side as Laura stepped cautiously down the gangplank with Dad behind her, his tweed fedora protecting his vulnerable bald spot. Behind them stood Mom in a sleeveless blue-and-white sundress.

Waiting for them to emerge from the ramshackle shed marked CUSTOMS in bold black letters, I prayed Dad wouldn't put René on the spot the minute they met. Although bold at home, Dad could turn shy in social situations, which sometimes came across as condescending. It had been known to happen with previous boyfriends. Once, he had greeted a boyfriend of Naomi's by asking if he was *extant*—as in, "Good evening, young man. Are you extant?" Not having the faintest idea what the word meant, the poor boy had squirmed and stuttered. The story had been immortalized in family history as an example of Dad at his *nadir* (another of his favorite words).

But René had reassured me when I'd warned him Dad might be awkward.

"Don't worry, it will all right," he said, omitting the "be."

With René's irrepressible optimism, it seemed that all things would miraculously be "all right." Still, I worried about how Dad would handle his fractured English. I expected to be doing a lot of interpreting to smooth their conversations.

My fears temporarily dissolved in the hugs we shared as soon as my parents emerged from customs without any scenes of scofflaw sailors or contraband jeans as when I'd first arrived.

"Welcome!" boomed René, his voice rising in direct proportion to his excitement.

With outstretched arms, René sprang to embrace my father, but taken by surprise, Dad offered his hand. Switching gears, René seized his hand but shook it so hard that Dad stumbled backward almost losing his balance. Teetering back and forth, they danced a bumbling jig like two clowns stepping on each other's toes—in more ways than one.

But René's enthusiasm remained undampened. "Pleased to meet you, Dr. Wagner!"

"Uh, you too, young man," stammered Dad, struggling to regain his composure.

The scene would have been hilarious if I hadn't been so mortified. How little they had in common! Technically they were both secular Jews, but the similarities stopped there. René's Jewish identity—a mishmash of Old World Ashkenazi and Sephardic customs inherited from his parents—contrasted wildly with Dad's "lite" brand of Reform Judaism, which he barely practiced. While Dad spoke English and the Hoch Deutsch he'd inherited from his mother, René spoke French and Hebrew. Neither of them spoke Yiddish. While Dad was a second-generation American music professor, René was the first-generation son of unschooled working-class immigrants. Where René was exuberant, my father was reserved. By any stretch of the imagination, they had next to nothing in common.

Hoping to right this gauche beginning, I introduced my mother.

"Enchanté!" beamed René, regaining his aplomb and kissing her on both cheeks in the French custom. She blushed, clearly charmed.

"And who is this petite *demoiselle?*" he cooed to Laura, trilling the "r" in lo-ra and boosting my little sister high in the air.

When it was Gidon's turn, he and Dad shook hands without incident, though Dad was clearly appraising the rumpled blue work clothes, mud-caked boots, and stubbled chin of this wiry farm worker who looked older than he expected. Apparently Gidon hadn't had time to shower or change after his shift at the refet. Still, Dad wasn't one to judge on appearances. Despite his own education, he had a deep respect for manual labor.

Although René wasn't one to shy away from hard work, he believed in working to live rather than living to work. His favorite motto in Hebrew was "slowly, slowly in the morning, not too fast in the afternoon." Accordingly, we'd spend a restful Shabbat with Naomi and Gidon in Hazorea before going to Haifa that Sunday morning—a workday in Israel.

By now the noonday heat and humidity had risen to stifling levels. Sweat was pouring off Dad's temples, Mom was wilting like an English rose, and Laura's cheeks were flushed. Jon shifted from one foot to the other, shading his eyes from the glare.

"'Ave you eaten lunch yet?" asked René, dropping the "h" in have with his French accent. "We must break bread together on this special occasion, non?"

"Sorry," declined Gidon. "I have to get back to work." By Naomi's look of disappointment, I knew she felt slighted.

Nudging Gidon aside, René hissed in his ear in rapid-fire Hebrew.

"*Ma, ata meshugah?* What, are you crazy? Relax, man! You can't leave without sharing lunch with your new family. Your sacred cows aren't mooing for you yet. The two p.m. bus will get you home before they finish chewing their cud."

With that, René hustled us all out into the grimy street where a teeming crowd instantly engulfed us. Aggressive vendors with rickety pushcarts hawked fly-blown bagels, salt-laden pretzels, and gray hunks of roasted *shwarma* (spicy slabs of beef). The tantalizing aroma mixed with the fumes of idling diesel engines. Jon seemed amused, but Dad's jaw was clenched and Mom's face had turned ashen. Laura clung to my arm for dear life.

"Come inside," commanded René, steering us into a café that was only slightly cooler and quieter than the chaos outdoors.

"Whew, what a maelstrom!" muttered Dad, collapsing into a chair at the head of a table covered in a red-and-white checked oilcloth.

"Bedlam!" said Mom—her English term for a madhouse.

"Cacophony!" declared Naomi.

"Mayhem!" I added.

Relieved that our sense of humor was still intact, my spirits rose when the waiter delivered a traditional Mediterranean spread—what else but hummus, baba ganoush, olives, dolmas, falafel, cucumber-tomato salad, and pita? Jon and Laura tried orange Fanta, while the rest of us ordered cool, fresh-squeezed grapefruit juice. Feeling better, Dad loosened his belt, wiped his mustache, and took a deep breath.

"You remind me of my own papa after a good meal," said René. "Ready for a nap now?"

But Dad squared his shoulders and flared his nostrils to show he still had energy to spare.

"Well then, we'd better get going if we want to catch the last bus for Kibbutz Dan," René said. The intricate meanings of Dad's Big Sniff were lost on him.

At the Central Bus Station we shared sweaty hugs with Naomi and Gidon before they left for Hazorea, taking Jonathan with them for his second week in Israel. Our plan was to show my parents around Galilee for their first week, then bring them back to Hazorea for a second week of sightseeing with Naomi and Gidon. In this way they'd get to know where we both lived as well as see a good part of northern and central Israel. With sizzling temperatures in August, we ruled out the Negev, especially given Dad's extreme sensitivity to heat. His pink skin and bald pate were no match for the merciless sun.

As the bus rolled north, Mom said the parched landscape reminded her of Texas, the first place Dad had found a job after bringing her to the US. For a girl from foggy London who spoke the king's English, the extreme heat and southern drawl had been a shock. Without a car, we had ridden the still-segregated buses. At four, Naomi and I had loved sitting on their bumpy back benches, but Mom didn't have the heart to tell us they were for "Negroes Only," so after awhile we had simply walked to the Piggly Wiggly for our groceries—boycotting the buses long before the Civil Rights Movement that was gaining momentum once again in the 1960s.

This bus ride would be the first of many for my parents in Israel. Hitchhiking wasn't an option for them, and renting a car would have been too expensive, so they would have to see the Land of Milk and Honey through the dusty windows of an Egged bus. But traveling by bus would also give them a firsthand glimpse of the diverse humanity I had come to love in Israel—from bearded Orthodox Jews in black coats and yarmulkes, to kibbutzniks in blue denim work shorts, to squawking chickens that occasionally flapped through the aisles until their no-nonsense owners recaptured them. As always, a few Arab men fingered prayer beads half hidden in the folds of their robes. I had warned my parents and Laura to be careful of the pyramids of spit-out sunflower husks left under the seats by previous passengers, despite signs that said No Cracking of Sunflower Seeds. Mom and Dad surveyed the scene with admirable serenity. I didn't dare ask what they thought of the bus driver's Uzi slung casually around the back of his seat.

Chapter 30

SIGHTSEEING IN THE UPPER GALILEE

Despite his political reservations about Israel, Dad found everything about kibbutz life intriguing, especially the socialized division of labor. True to Avram Fein's prediction long ago, Mom loved the concept of the collective dining room where she wouldn't have to cook a single meal—unless, of course, she was assigned to work in the kitchen! They weren't so sure about the *bet yelidim*, where children slept in the care of a *mitapelet* (caregiver) rather than at home, but they couldn't refute how boisterous and happy the kids looked. Maybe a degree of family separation was for the best. But what about babies, Mom wanted to know? Wouldn't their mothers want them nearby instead of getting up at all hours to nurse them in the *bet tinokot* (baby house)? I hadn't considered this inconvenience, so I had no answer, but Dad chimed in with Avram's famous remark about every problem having a soluuuu-tion. I dreaded telling him that Avram didn't remember saying this himself, but Dad would find out in due time when we visited Ein Hashofet the following week. I only hoped my encounter with the Feins wouldn't be too strained.

Although René had to work that week, I'd been lucky enough to get time off to spend with my family, since I was technically a volunteer. I had a full itinerary planned. Some of the sites were on or near the kibbutz, like Beit Ussishkin, a hard-to-pronounce natural museum. Mom pored over displays of native plants and animals from biblical times while Jon studied the artifacts from the Hellenic Period. Was there no end to the successive invasions of this land?

"That guy Pan must have been quite the hell-raiser with his cloven hooves and devil's tail," Jon mused, inducting the Greek god of debauchery into his personal Pantheon.

"Does his pipe make him the original Pied Piper?" added Dad.

At Tel Dan, Jon soaked his swollen feet in the bubbling headwaters, relieving the blisters from his work boots. I unstrapped my sandals and let the icy water flow between my toes. The mingling of hot air and frigid liquid sent molten shivers up my legs until my whole body shuddered with delight. But Dad couldn't be coaxed to expose his feet and give it a try. We teased him for being a tenderfoot. Although he prized physical stamina, even on the beach at home he wore socks and shoes to protect his delicate feet.

With only a week ahead, I was eager to show my family as much as possible of my new home in the Hula Valley of the Upper Galilee. Unlike the south of Israel, water in the north was surprisingly abundant. I explained that Hula Valley had been a malarial swamp until it was drained for agriculture in the 1950s. Most people were proud of this transformation, but some had worried. The valley was also a flyway for thousands of migrating birds from the Great Rift in Africa along the Syrian axis. A fierce debate now raged between the supporters of development and those urging preservation.

"Just like logging the redwoods at home," Dad said. The lumber trucks that clogged Highway 101 seemed far away, but the comparison was all too close.

"I hope they create a wildlife refuge," said Mom. My mother loved birds. She often said she wanted to be one in her next life.

"You'll see a beautiful preserve tomorrow," I answered. The sudden image of my mother fleeing a chicken coop or bursting out of a gilded cage caught me off guard. What was wrong with me today? I couldn't seem to shake a wicked sense of humor. Perhaps she'd be a pink flamingo, a ruby-throated humming-bird, a robin redbreast, or even a rare cockatoo. Who knew? I only knew that no matter how far my mother and I traveled apart in this life or the next, she would always be with me. Even if, in the dim future, I took on the foolhardy task of writing a book, her spirit would be there to guide my heart, hand, and head to *just* the right word. Now the words she had spoken when I was only seven floated back to me like a command or a prophesy, I wasn't sure which: "You should write."

Horshat Tal, a national park that had recently been cre-ated to preserve the fabled cold springs and gigantic trees there since biblical times, was a short bus ride away, so I packed a picnic lunch in the kibbutz kitchen—the usual mix of bread, sardines, cucumbers, tomatoes, hard-boiled eggs, some slices of white cheese, and a bunch of ripe grapes—and we set off.

Laura was the first to notice the rows of olives trees that lined both sides of the road that led from the kibbutz to the highway. "What kind of trees have such gnarledy old trunks and feathery gray-green leaves?" she asked.

Like a budding professor, Jonathan launched into a lengthy lesson on "The History of the Olive in the Middle East," which Laura tried hard to process. Then it was my turn to add what I knew of the trees today. Rumor had it that every year in Novem-ber, when the olive harvest season began, the kibbutz would allow the neighboring Druze villagers to pick what had been theirs in the first place, before the state of Israel had expropriated their land after the war of '48. The kibbutz felt this was only fair and just.

"I wonder how the villagers feel about that?" asked Dad.

I said we couldn't really know unless we went to the village to ask them, but that would be impossible because, although the Druze were known for their unswerving loyalty to Israel, going to a village uninvited was essentially taboo.

"That's too bad," Dad replied pensively, though his brown eyes suggested far more. If the eyes are truly the windows to the soul (as Mom liked to quote Shakespeare), then the subtle shadings of Dad's eyes—from coffee to russet, to bronze or burnt ochre, could convey a full range of emotion without his ever uttering a word. But the fine art of reading my father's eyes was always touch and go for a girl of words like me. If only we shared a common language!

That day, however, Dad's eyes told me precisely what he was thinking. And sadly, I had to admit he had a point: that for all its lofty ideals, Israel was a segregated society where Jewish and Arab citizens lived side by side yet attended separate schools and enjoyed unequal rights; where, despite the promise of equality, fear, mutual ignorance, and discrimination ruled most relations between two groups who each loved the land with a passion. In Dad's eyes, the society bore an uncanny resemblance to the relations of Blacks and whites in the American South of the early sixties. These were not the Jewish values he had instilled in us, his children. But in my single-focused zeal to help build the new socialist state, I had overlooked (or rationalized) these deep inequities.

Just then the bus pulled to a halt, abruptly ending our conversation as we reached Horshat Tal. I could think of nothing more to say on such a sensitive and complicated subject anyway. Still, I knew there would come a time when I wouldn't be able to ignore the thorny question of Palestinian rights.

Peeling our damp derrières from the sticky plastic seats, we stepped off the bus and into a world of gurgling waterways, grassy grounds, and an inviting man-made swimming pool. Jon insisted on stopping to read all the English inscriptions on the many signs along the way, reveling in the park's biblical and historical background.

"Look, Dad," I pointed out. "All the signs are in Arabic and English, as well as Hebrew." At least there was an effort toward equality. One marker said the trees were over seven hundred years old; another cited a biblical account of the ancient oak trees:

> *Legend has it that one of the huge Tavor oaks in the park had been split in two by a huge earthquake in the eighth century. But managing to heal its wounds, it grew into two separate trees joined at the roots.*

We stopped to gaze at the conjoined roots of two massive trunks whose branches met in a graceful arch overhead. Could the relationship Naomi and I shared withstand such a riveting, I wondered, yet stay forever connected at our shared roots? The question made me realize that I'd come to feel less worried about surviving outside our twin bubble than I had a year earlier. Step by step, I was becoming more independent. But more ominously, would my family survive the split that would soon follow this calm visit? In two weeks we'd be waving goodbye as they sailed home on the same ship that had taken Naomi and me away.

At the swimming pool a sign warned that the water temperature was a glacial twelve degrees Celsius (fifty-five degrees Fahrenheit) all year round, but by now I was sweltering in the heat and nothing could keep me from plunging in. Curling my toes on the lip of the high-dive board, I stretched my arms overhead in a V shape and arched my back in preparation for a perfect swan dive, secretly hoping to impress my father. Dad had taught Naomi and me to swim when we were barely three, and since then I'd been a water dog. I still recalled my joy (and his shock) when, at age eight I'd beaten him in an underwater race. The feel of the silken water gliding over my body as I darted to the finish line had been as delicious as my unexpected victory while Dad was still churning through the pool like a whale in a bathtub. A champion in baseball and football, his thick limbs made for clumsy swimming.

Thwack! The icy water hit my head with the force of a hammer almost knocking me out. Heaving for breath, I hauled myself to the surface and sprawled out on the lawn. The sun stabbed my skin like a thousand needles. Nursing my wounded pride as well as my smarting head, I was relieved the lifeguard—if there was one—hadn't noticed me any more than Dad. I said nothing of my queasiness, much less my pounding headache, as we ate our lunch and dabbled in the shallow streams beneath the giant oaks for the rest of the afternoon. But the next morning, I woke up with a raging cold. Still, not wanting my ill-fated swan dive to spoil our happiness at Horshat Tal, I didn't complain. I would be Dad's big, strong girl if it killed me! Besides, the visit was going swimmingly, and I wanted it to stay that way.

At the end of each excursion, René would join us for supper after his tough workday. As expected, I played the part of interpreter, smoothing out the communication when it got hopelessly bogged down in three languages. Dad was clearly impressed by my growing command of Hebrew and French, and his respect for René seemed to be growing, too. The more he learned of our plans—working in the family market business in France before returning to Israel to continue our education—the more reasonable he found them. Still, it was odd to feel Dad passing the baton—or more precisely, relinquishing his authority to René—like a feudal lord bestowing his daughter on a worthy suitor. What seemed most important to Dad was whether René could take good care of me. That a young woman might manage alone in the world without a man was still a remote concept in the early sixties. If Dad prized the intellectual independence of his wife and daughters, he never questioned his role as traditional male provider, a double message that unwittingly fostered emotional and economic dependence. I wondered if that was why my mother fantasized becoming a bird, free of Dad's dominion. Or perhaps she simply yearned to fly home to her family. Much as I craved his love, I was desperate to fly free in order to make a life for myself.

The last stop on our sightseeing marathon was the town of Tiberias, also known as Tiveria, on the slopes of the Sea of Galilee, also known as the Kinneret. Every place in Israel went by multiple names and spellings, connoting the conquerors of the times. Scouring a guidebook, Jon was thrilled to discover that Tiberias had been founded in 20 CE in honor of a Roman emperor, although earliest evidence of habitation dated back to the Bronze Age. He recited the various periods of rule over the town from the earliest eras to modern times: "Jewish Biblical, Herodian, Roman, Byzantine, Early Muslim, Crusader, Mameluke, Ottoman, British Mandate, and last but not least, the state of Israel. Hey, it also says that Tiberias is the lowest city in Israel at 200 feet below sea level."

"What about the Dead Sea?" challenged Laura. "Isn't that the lowest place on earth?"

"Well, it may be the lowest *point* on the planet," answered Jon with authority, "but there's no actual city there."

"Well, I beg to differ," sniffed Dad. "Jericho, which is close to the Dead Sea, albeit in Jordan, is supposed to be the longest continuously inhabited town in the world."

"I'm sure you're each right in your own ways," interjected Mom, attempting to keep our differences from turning into an argument.

"And isn't the Sea of *Galilee* where Jesus walked on water and turned it into wine?" added Laura, with equal authority.

To avoid the worst of the day's heat, we had arrived early enough to visit the ruins of a two-thousand-year-old Roman theatre and admire the town's unique black-and-white basalt buildings before relaxing in the warm waters of the Kinneret, on the western side of the Upper Galilee's brown hills. Although larger than Eilat, Tiberias was still a small enclave, devoid of the high-rises, hotels, and apartments slated to climb its hills.

Hungry for lunch, we followed the tantalizing scent of sizzling falafel to an outdoor stand where a curly-haired young vendor was juggling balls of chickpea paste high in the air, then deftly catching them in pockets of pita bread as if they were baseball mitts. The show wowed us all. Mom was initially wary of the spicy saucy condiments as I rolled their names my tongue—*pilpelim* (peppers), *chamutzim* (pickles), and *chatzilim* (eggplant)—but like a stalwart Englishwoman, she gave them a try. By two p.m. it was time to catch the last bus to Haifa, and from there to Hazorea in time for Erev Shabbat.

Back in Hazorea, Gidon would take over as tour guide for the second week, a role he loved. Meanwhile, René and I needed to return to Kibbutz Dan for work. But this created a huge dilemma—we wouldn't have time to go to Ein Hashofet. To solve the problem, I asked Gidon and Naomi to arrange a visit for my parents with the Feins. I couldn't cope with the guilt if they didn't at least share a cup of tea after coming all this way. But I also couldn't deny my immense relief that I wouldn't be there for a second grilling, or smile away the stress I had caused in their long friendship.

Unlike Kibbutz Dan, Hazorea had a swimming pool. After our busy week of sightseeing, I imagined Mom and Dad would be more than happy to relax under a canopy there while Jon and Laura splashed in the water. But Jon was also eager to see the archeological ruins of Megiddo, not far from

Hazorea, where the fate of nations had been decided in many biblical battles. It was also associated with Armageddon, whose mystery enthralled him. And I knew Gidon had a long list of other points of interest—the natural pools at Gan Ha'Shlosha, a hike on Mount Tabor, the Roman ruins at Beit She'an, and the Baha'i Temple in Haifa with its gleaming gold dome, to name only a few in the Jezreel Valley and Lower Galilee. His only problem would be taking time off from the refet.

The sheer number of ruins, ramparts, castles, dungeons, Roman theatres, and Byzantine mosaics unearthed in such a small country was dizzying—and more were constantly being discovered. Like amateur archaeologists, my family had been fascinated by Israel. Their fears had subsided as they experienced the reality of our lives in this new land. Having added their own footprints to the historical record, they would carry home a context for our lives in Israel.

Beit Ushishkin at Kibbutz Dan

René, Paula, Jean and Laura, Kibbutz Dan, 1964

Horshat Tal National Park

Gidon, Naomi, Jon, Laura and Jean at the Pool at Hazorea

Chapter 31

WINNING AND LOSING

The two weeks of my family's visit flew by until all too soon, the day of departure arrived. Once again we journeyed to the sweltering port of Haifa. We no longer talked about when or whether Naomi and I would accompany them home.

"How can you bear this awful heat?" my mother asked irritably. "It's as bad as Texas." She'd braved Israel's roiling dust and roasting temperatures for as long as she could, but now I sensed her urgency to escape. Whereas Israel reminded me of the climate I'd loved as a little girl, my mother had suffered asthma attacks and exhaustion in Texas. Iowa and Kansas hadn't been much better. After a decade of moving across the US, she had been only too happy to settle on the foggy coast of Northern California. Now our longings for escape were reversed.

Nevertheless, I could hardly bear the sight of my parents boarding the *Theodore Herzl*. Mom made a show of waving bravely, as her own mother must have done, while Dad hid his grief behind a camera, snapping photos of the daughters he was losing.

Despite how articulate we were as a family, we had failed to find a common language to bridge our differences. Our paths had long since diverged toward separate horizons. And so, although there had been ample opportunity during my parents' visit in Israel, we had carefully avoided any meaningful conversation. Mom, Dad, Jon, and Laura would journey home, while Naomi and I stayed in Israel. If our parents hadn't fully accepted our decision, at least they had acquiesced.

It would be years before I saw the photos of their journey home. In one, Naomi and I appear to be smiling as we wave from the dock, while René and Gidon stand behind us with their hands on our shoulders. In another, taken in the ship's mess hall, Dad sports a jaunty smile, as if trying to desperately assuage Mom's misery. But my mother's gaze is distant. In truth, they both look shell-shocked by events they could neither foresee nor forestall. Other pictures show them smiling at the pool in Hazorea. In another, my mother looks impossibly young standing next to Laura and me, on Kibbutz Dan.

As the ship's cable uncoiled like the fraying bonds of my family, I too felt unmoored. Love, loss, grief, and relief clamored like wild children in my chest. If only I could fly after the ship like an albatross! Finally, burying my head in René's chest, I let my tears flow.

"*Ne pleure pas, Chèrie*—don't cry," he comforted. "It will all right."

Like a river breaching a sandbar to the sea, my heart emptied out at last. In the void that gaped open, an unfamiliar power rose within me. The mournful bellow of the ship's horn now rang like a clarion. Free! I was free at last from Dad's control! Independent and on my own!

Still, my newfound freedom had come at a huge cost. Suddenly my happiest childhood memories of Dad lay like limp toy soldiers slain on the battlefield of my rebellion: Memories of happier times came flooding back—camping trips in the redwoods; Dad composing a new piece on the piano late at night; snowball fights in Iowa; rescuing a box turtle from a road that cut through shimmering cottonwoods in Kansas; hunting for prized agates at the tideline of a beach in California; summer trips to the annual Shakespeare Festival in Oregon. But like a phantom, my childhood had suddenly sailed away.

I had come to Israel in search of my father's roots, but also to slip his control. I had come on a quest for my freedom, but now I had lost him—if indeed I had ever been sure of him. Separating from my mother and even Naomi felt different—a sad but necessary transition. The love at the core of those relationships would endure over time and space, of that I was sure. But Dad's love seemed bound up in approval ratings, something to be earned or achieved, never unconditionally bestowed. At school, at home, or at the piano—would I ever be accomplished enough to deserve his love?

All the way back to Dan, my emotions lurched and jostled with every hairpin turn on the tortuous road. But by the time we reached the gates of the kibbutz, my grief had turned to gritty determination. Paradoxically, I had needed a hot, harsh land to dry up all my tears. A land whose people had endured hardships far beyond my own and yet survived. A land where my sensitive soul—my *nefesh adina*—could grow strong and resilient, like the vines in the kerem. No longer the dejected girl I'd been in the fog of Arcata, I'd gained a sense of purpose and identity through my struggle to learn the language and adapt to an unfamiliar culture. In the span of ten short months, I'd moved light years beyond the confining comfort of my family, too far to turn back now. Besides, I liked this new me much better than the old doubt-plagued self that I'd shed like a husk. By the time we reached Dan, I strode decisively through its gates and into my new life.

Naomi, Gidon, Paula and René, Waving Farewell in Haifa

Jean, Leon, Jon and Laura, Homeward Bound

PART IV

ISRAEL—FALL 1964

Chapter 32

NAOMI'S WEDDING

The day promised to be warm and sunny for Naomi and Gidon's wedding to be held on Shabbat at Kibbutz Hazorea in late September of 1964. René and I had made the long trip from Dan with a stop in Haifa, then narrowly caught the last bus to Hazorea before all public transit ceased on Friday for Erev Sabbath. Initially, René had favored hitchhiking to save what little money we had for our upcoming trip to France. But I had argued that the roads would surely be clogged with soldiers hitchhiking home for Shabbat and we might be stranded for hours. We had lots of pre-travel business to take care of before our trip to France and couldn't afford to waste time waiting for a ride. The ferry ticket office and the bank would gobble up most of our time before they pulled down their shutters at noon or at the latest two. With everyone else rushing to finish their business before the Sabbath, Friday lines were always long. The last bus for Hazorea was at three, and we couldn't afford to miss it. We argued the pros and cons of hitchhiking versus taking the bus until I was almost in tears. At last René had relented, but the stress of our squabble had tinged my excitement for what was supposed to be a special occasion. Boarding the early morning bus under a cloud, I hoped my mood would improve for the wedding.

As I approached the dining room to meet Naomi for breakfast that Saturday morning, the sounds and sights of wedding preparations were already in full swing. On the wide lawn outside the hadar ha'ochel, several men were hammering in the last nails of a large platform—the *bima*. Next, a crew of women swooped in to sheathe it in sheets of white. The men then set six sets of folding chairs in a wide semicircle and added a wooden podium. Someone was testing a microphone, hooked up to endless extension cords. The only thing conspicuously absent from the preparations were any religious symbols. Not even a *chupa*—the traditional canopy held over the bride and groom—graced the platform. This was to be a completely secular celebration.

Inside the dining room, small vases of colorful flowers adorned the white cloths on at least fifty tables. To one side, two men were reaching precariously from the platform of a large indoor crane, trying to tack rainbow streamers to the ceiling. When the silky panels slipped from their hands, people below gathered them up and cheered them on. Although it was still breakfast, the garlicky scent of chicken soup and spices—cumin, cardamom, and cinnamon—told me the cooks were already hard at work preparing a wedding feast for hundreds of guests.

In the collective tradition of the kibbutz, Naomi and Gidon would not be celebrating this festive occasion alone, but sharing it with five other couples who would join them in the semicircle on the outdoor stage before family and friends. Many were already streaming in from neighboring kibbutzim, towns, and villages. Others had arrived the day before.

Although the ceremony wouldn't happen until four in the afternoon, after the heat of the day had subsided, the kibbutz buzzed with growing anticipation. But the time seemed interminable to Naomi. I tried to calm her with small talk, but she seemed in a daze.

"You're in a *brown study*," I said, using our mother's quirky English expression for daydreaming.

"What?"

"You're in a daze," I repeated, cajoling her gently back to earth. "Remember how Mom used to say that when we were kids and we thought it was so weird?"

Although I had no idea where the expression came from, my memory of it was suffused with a warm and fuzzy quality—like the muted light that filtered through my mother's amber pendant at the neck of the velveteen dress she had worn for poetry recitals when we were eight; or simply like the comforting taste of a cup of milky tea.

"Oh yes," laughed Naomi at last, only to lapse back into a *brown study* that seemed more blue than brown.

I hoped I hadn't inadvertently opened the door to Naomi's nostalgia too. Was she missing Mom as much as I on this occasion? While there would be hundreds of guests on the lawn, our parents would not be among them. With Dad's sabbatical at an end, they could afford neither the time nor the money to return so soon from California. In fact, I would be my sister's only next of kin.

Who was absent from weddings in my family defined our tradition at least as much as who was present. Because our parents had married as bombs still fell on London in 1944, our grandparents had been unable to come from Chicago for their wedding. It was doubtful my parents would be able to attend my marriage ceremony in France. Flying halfway around the world, even for a wedding, was simply too expensive for most people in the sixties.

However, Naomi and I would not be the only ones without family for the occasion. Gidon's mother would not be flying in from Toronto in Canada either. And his father, having died in the Holocaust, would be present only in spirit. Gidon was the last surviving male in his generation. The community of kibbutz members, friends, and army buddies would have to stand in for the lack of blood relatives.

By three-thirty, the hushed excitement of waiting gave way to a growing wave of laughter and chatter as guests crowded into a sea of folding chairs below the *bima* on the lawn. Men had exchanged their blue work overalls for black pants and white shirts open at the collar (no ties). Women had traded in their weekly brown garb for colorful Shabbat skirts and dresses. Store-bought sandals replaced the heavy leather kibbutz variety. Children shouted and turned cartwheels when not darting between the legs of grown-ups. Everyone looked scrubbed and combed as friends and family embraced until the low chatter rose to a roar.

When everyone was finally seated, a string quartet played a classical adagio and the crowd grew calmer. The celebration was beginning. A duo of guitarists led the group in some traditional songs such as "Hine Ma Tov U Manayim"—How good it is for brothers to gather together. In place of a rabbi, the kibbutz president made some announcements, then gave a brief secular blessing, congratulated the couples on behalf of the entire kibbutz, and wished them well.

When it was their turn, each couple rose to read a psalm or short piece, chosen more as poetry than for piety. Although she sat among five other couples, Naomi was the only bride I observed. From my vantage point below, I could see a poised figure in a sleek crepe gown, accented only by the thin gold necklace and modest pearl eardrops that I'd given her.

I wondered how she saw what I was seeing. Later she would describe it as a summery scene of upturned heads swiveling over a checkerboard sea of black and white in a bright floral garden. She would also tell me that she felt swept along by a future beyond her control. That she had felt herself becoming small and invisible, floating like a bubble on a river. That, like me, she was becoming a new person with a new language and culture, while her old American self faded away. But while I had welcomed this transformation, she had experienced it more like a hijacking of her former self. The collective pressures and rewards of kibbutz life were as seductive as the arms that had drawn her into it.

But I knew nothing of this as I played the role of loyal sister. A part of me longed to sit on the *bima* beside René, as Naomi now sat next to Gidon. Then they would be our guests. But kibbutz weddings were for members only, and René and I were not planning to become members of Kibbutz Dan. A kibbutz wedding was a public covenant signifying a commitment to the group that was as strong or stronger than the bond between spouses. Only individuals deemed likely to contribute to the collective good would rate a ceremony, but even divorced couples could still stay on as members. The kibbutz would simply give them separate rooms. The personal and the political were inextricably intertwined.

Beyond the secular kibbutzim, marriage was even more complicated in Israeli society at large, where the Orthodox rabbis decreed that only if the mothers of both partners were Jewish, could they be legally married. Without the option of a civil union, people like me were barred from officially marrying. Despite the consternation of the Orthodox Rabbinate, the secular kibbutz movement took pride in conducting their own ceremonies, effectively circumventing the law. Even if kibbutz weddings like Naomi and Gidon's weren't officially legal, they were socially recognized as equally binding.

✧ ✧

At the dining hall, a band struck up with the feverish tunes of Klezmer, the traditional folk music of Eastern Europe, on a clarinet and fiddles as the sound system screeched to life. Children raced among servers and guests with abandon. In the chaos, I hugged Naomi and Gidon and wished them the customary mazel tov. Naomi smiled, her mask of composure intact.

"*Ochel, ochel,*" chanted the crowd, "bring on the food." Bottles of Maccabee beer and fruit juice popped, husks of sunflower seeds and pits of black and green olives began piling into pyramids. The *chamutzim* (pickled vegetables) were long gone by the time the main fare arrived: bowls of steaming chicken soup and matzo balls, fish, chicken, beef, roast potatoes, cabbage, and gravy washed down with tomato-cucumber-chopped-parsley salad.

Suddenly I missed my mother intensely. If only she could be here! I could just imagine her taking in the scene with wry humor: *devouring everything like locusts . . . with the appetite of Falstaff,* in an incongruous mix of Shakespeare and Jewish tradition.

Golden sheet cakes inscribed with good wishes in lemon and blue frosting were cut into squares and served with strawberries and whipped cream, along with trays of baklava, blintzes, and cinnamon twists. There was no shortage of food—God forbid! If the ceremony had been unconventional, the wedding feast rolled out in full Jewish traditional. While Jews might "argue the hind legs off a donkey"—another of Mom's favorite English sayings—they could almost always agree on food!

As the dishes were being cleared away, René stepped outside to smoke a Gaulois. He urged Gidon to join him.

"C'mon, man. Time to celebrate with a *real* cigarette." He took a deep drag and exhaled, swirling the fumes into the cool evening air.

He'd bought a pack of Gauloises especially for the occasion. Even if they were considerably more expensive, French cigarettes were far better than the sawdust-tasting kibbutz brands. I didn't smoke because of my allergies, but in those days almost everyone did, so I didn't think to protest.

When all the tables and chairs had been pushed to the walls, the *Klezmer* band coaxed the crowd onto the floor. Grinning proudly, Gidon strode to the center, linked arms with the dancers of his kibbutz troupe, and launched the rikudei am—folk dances—into motion. The audience roared as he twisted his athletic body like a pretzel, whirled in circles, squatted at the knees, and kicked out his legs like a Russian Cossack.

Guests and families widened the circle until the entire hall became a spinning mass of humanity. I tried not to step on any toes, but compared with René and Gidon, I felt clumsy. The melee continued until little by little the group thinned, leaving only the hardiest still upright. But there was no slow dancing. Like suits and ties, social dancing in pairs was seen as anticollective and bourgeois.

By midnight the festivities began to wind down. With their promises sealed and celebrated, the lives of the new couples would merge like rivers. My feelings for Naomi ricocheted from glad to sad to happy to worried. In Israel, we had taken our first steps toward autonomy. Now, in a few short weeks, I'd be far away in France, making an even greater leap into the uncharted territory of independence. Without phones, much less social media, to bridge the continents, cultures, and languages between us, we would be forced to follow our separate paths to an unknown future.

Gidon wanted a few last dances with his group, but Naomi was exhausted, so I accompanied her back to their room. Unzipping her dress, she peeled the pearly bodice over her breasts and let out her tummy. Then she bent to loosen the straps of her white sandals. Her usually slim figure filled out the contours of the dress a tad tighter than when she had tried it on in England.

"You looked lovely, Nento!" I said, suppressing my lingering envy of her dress. "How do you feel now?"

"Okay, I guess." But the flatness in her voice and the slump of her shoulders told otherwise. "Maybe I'm just tired."

"Is anything wrong?"

"Really nothing. I'll be okay by tomorrow, I promise."

Silence. Then, forcing back tears, Naomi drew in her breath and blurted out what I already suspected. "I might as well tell you. I'm six weeks pregnant."

I had squelched my intuition, but now the telltale signs of her body could no longer be denied.

"I didn't want to get pregnant! But all the birth control methods I've tried have failed. The pill makes me sick, and the damn diaphragm obviously isn't reliable."

In the early sixties, the pill had only recently become available, but the estrogen dosages were so high that many women couldn't tolerate it. I stood in silence as she spilled out her worries.

"I can't have another abortion. Last spring was too horrible."

"I know," I said simply, wincing at the memory of that awful day. Afterward, I had tried to console her, but she had pushed me away in her own attempt to stay strong. Just when I yearned to hold her close, she had held me at bay. My own hurt and confusion had twisted into a tangle of resentment and sorrow. The pattern had dogged us since childhood. Now I agonized for Naomi but stood back, afraid my comfort might deflate the day's joy beyond repair. But the illusion of a happily-ever-after wedding had tumbled to the floor with her dress.

Abortion was a gray area—neither strictly legal nor illegal—in Israel at the time but left to personal discretion (or indiscretion) of each woman. But with birth control still spotty, unplanned pregnancies were hard to prevent. Still, I wondered how I had managed to avoid getting pregnant when my twin sister had been betrayed by her fertility. But at twenty-nine, I imagined Gidon was eager to start a family, especially as the sole surviving male member of his family. Besides his mother, he had virtually no other relatives. The Holocaust had claimed them all. Without children, his name would die out. I had heard him joke darkly that having children would be his revenge on Hitler.

Hugging Naomi good night, I made my way back to the small guest room provided by the kibbutz. René was fast asleep, to judge by his snoring. Rocking gently on the porch swing outside the bedroom, I let my thoughts wander under the waning moon. Naomi's revelation had left a bittersweet residue on the events of the day, entangling my heart with joy and regret like the vines in the kerem. I hoped the fruit of Naomi and Gidon's union would be as sweet as the grapes I had harvested on Kibbutz Dan once the bitterness had passed.

Chapter 33

RENÉ'S COUSINS

Before leaving for France, René wanted to introduce me and also say his goodbyes to some of his many cousins who also lived in Israel. Having grown up together in a large extended clan in postwar Lyon, they had formed strong bonds. After hearing some of their childhood stories, I was eager to meet them.

Five of the cousins were sisters whose father had been deported during WWII. When he failed to return after the war, their mother (René's father's sister) was left to raise them alone. Although no one knew for sure what had happened to him, they had pieced together a sad but likely scenario from the vague reports of other survivors. Apparently, when the Russian and American troops had converged on his camp at liberation, he had sided with the Russians. But their frigid march to the east had cost him his life. In a supreme irony, he had died, not because he was a Jew, but for his stalwart Socialist views.

Left to rely on her wits, René's aunt had become the matriarch of Lyon's fruit and vegetable marché. Rising at four a.m., she bargained for the best prices in the hurly-burly man's world of the wholesale market, long before setting up her stall within the neighborhood market with the help of her five daughters each morning. Despite the grueling work, the marché had been their salvation. Not only had it put food on the table, but it had kept a roof over their heads and clothes on their backs. But the struggle to survive had left little time for the cousins' education and limited opportunities for their future in France.

Seeking a better life, the five sisters had emigrated to Israel as part of Ha'Shomer Ha'Tzair, the Socialist Jewish youth movement that would have warmed their father's heart. Impressed by their experience, René had been inspired to follow. Now, having finished their compulsory military service, they were eager to launch their lives as full-fledged Israelis.

We had already visited Esther, the eldest of the five sister/cousins, and her husband, who had established themselves on Kibbutz Bar'am, which was not far from Kibbutz Dan and less than a quarter of a mile from the Lebanese border. If my memories of Esther are minimal, my impressions of her kibbutz remain vivid: Bar'am had been established in 1949 on the site of an ancient Jewish village, where over the centuries, a predominantly Maronite Christian village called K'far Bir'Im had grown up. To deter the frequent cross-border incursions at the time, the Israeli government had destroyed the village and expelled its inhabitants. As we surveyed the ruins, I couldn't help imagining its former inhabitants living in refugee camps just over the nearby border.

Like Dan, Kibbutz Bar'am grew a variety of crops, including apples, nectarines, plums, and even kiwis, that flourished in the hot, sunny days and cool, breezy nights of the Upper Galilee. And like the Syrian border, the tragic beauty of the Lebanese border both enthralled and disturbed me. Gazing over the expanse of fields and orchards, the border appeared both close and remote. Although my brain recognized the danger, in my heart I felt the pain of a deep unhealed scar, forever separating two peoples from the land they both loved.

Compared with the open vista and cool breezes of Bar'am, Netanya, a beach town near Tel Aviv, was humid and steamy even in October. When two of Esther's younger sisters—Rachel and Miriam—met us at the door of the small apartment they shared, I immediately noticed how much their large almond eyes and silver-streaked dark hair resembled René's traits from the Turkish side of the family. After customary kisses on both cheeks, they welcomed us into their modest living room.

"Coffee?"

"Of course!" boomed René. "What's a family visit without Turkish coffee?"

Miriam hurried to a small alcove that served as a kitchen while Rachel sat cross-legged on the rug-covered stone floor. Out of the corner of my eye, I watched Miriam move through the coffee-making ritual, step by step: setting a saucepan to boil on a hot plate; grinding the beans by hand and stirring the fine powder into the water along with a few pods of cardamom. As soon as bubbles simmered to the surface, she turned off the gas and covered the pot with a saucer to let the grounds settle. Finally, she poured the dark, thick liquid into four porcelain cups. Clearly Turkish coffee was to René's family what English tea was to mine.

Fueled by caffeine, René and his cousins caught up on each other's news in rapid-fire French, too fast for me to follow. But their English was even more limited, so I spent most of the afternoon nodding *oui* or *non*, in polite hopes of being right about 50 percent of the time.

Finally we switched to Hebrew for the sake of a common language around the supper table—a spread of hard-boiled eggs, hummus, pita, cottage cheese, olives, tomatoes, and cucumbers that I never tired of.

When night fell, Rachel apologized for their limited sleeping arrangements but quickly offered a solution.

"If René doesn't mind a mattress on the floor, Miriam and I are happy to share the double bed with Paula."

Seeing my puzzled look, she explained.

"That's how we used to sleep as kids in France—three to a bed head-to-toe. Look, we'll show you," she added when I still looked baffled.

Giggling like schoolgirls, Rachel wriggled under the quilt feetfirst, while Miriam dove in headlong, only to pop out like a puppet at the foot of the bed.

"There's still plenty of room in the middle for you Paula," they laughed. "Don't be shy—we're family."

With no choice but to squeeze into the narrow space like a sausage in a straitjacket, I crawled carefully between the cousins, trying to avoid kicking Rachel's head or tickling Miriam's feet. I had never shared a bed before, not even with Naomi. Squished so tightly together, I doubted I'd get much rest that night. But the arrangement wasn't as weird as I'd feared. Like a new patch on the family quilt—or at least under it—the cousins embraced me. If René's family was anywhere near as welcoming, I'd feel right at home in Lyon.

At first light the next morning, I untangled my arms and legs like a warm pretzel and inched out of bed, trying not to disturb Rachel and Miriam in their blissful slumber. I needn't have worried. They slept as deeply as René. After a simple breakfast of café au lait and a French baguette, we hugged goodbye. Then René and I caught the bus for Jerusalem, where we planned to visit Dafna, another cousin from yet another branch of René's far-flung family.

Chapter 34

EIN KEREM

J ust outside Jerusalem, the bus stopped in the scenic village
of Ein Kerem. Like Bar-am, it had been a Christian village
before its Palestinian inhabitants had fled (or were driven out)
in 1948. Its domed whitewashed homes, picturesque churches,
and a massive stone monastery—Notre Dame de Sion—now
provided the backdrop for an Israeli artists' colony in the making. Entranced, I followed René up a steeply winding path.

"Shalom, shalom!" called a woman with a heavy French
accent. Dafna had already spied us from her perch on her
vine-covered *mirpeset* (patio) high above a valley. Looking up,
I was greeted by a pair of almond eyes and a round, smiling face,
framed by a few stray strands of silver curling from the braided
coils of Dafna's henna-tinted hair. She was perhaps a year older
than I and I liked her immediately.

But at the top of the stone steps, our way was blocked by a
gaunt figure in mud-spattered overalls with a cigarette dangling
from his lips. Fully absorbed in cranking a portable cement mixer,
he barely looked up.

"Hey, Khanan!" yelled René over the din as the machine roared suddenly to life. Without pausing from his labors, Khanan grunted a belated *bonjour*. Luckily, René had already warned me that beneath his crusty manner, Khanan had a warm heart. Like René, Khanan had also grown up in the same gritty quartier of Lyon. Street urchins since childhood, they didn't stand on ceremony.

"Come in, come in!" bubbled Dafna, kissing us three times on each cheek, her sunshiny welcome dispelling Khanan's dark mood. They had moved in only recently. Evidence of multiple construction and art projects, piles of books, and tools lay everywhere.

"Sorry, everything is still so makeshift. We don't even have a real bathroom or kitchen yet. But as you can see, Khanan's in full building mode."

A tiny kitchen annex and bathroom were still works in progress behind a long enclosed porch. In the large main room, the arches of four walls met in the center of a high domed ceiling like graceful arms in prayer. The faded blue-and-yellow tiles on the floor under my feet felt smooth with age. Paintings, photos, and colorful mobiles—evidence of Khanan's creativity—cluttered the room. Perching on a narrow window seat in a recess of the thick exterior wall, I peered through two vaulted panes at the panoramic view of vineyards, terraced valleys, and forested hills far below. An agricultural school sat near a crossroads, and a cluster of red-tiled roofs signaled a *moshav*—a collective village.

Directing my attention to the left side of the valley, Khanan pointed out the skeleton of a massive modern building under construction, from the looks of its scaffolding and the huge steel girders suspended from swaying orange cranes. In the heat of the day, he was taking a break while the concrete set.

"That's Hadassah Hospital going up on that hill over there," he motioned proudly. "It's going to be the biggest, most modern hospital in all of Israel."

But cooing sounds diverted my attention to a cradle half-hidden in the chaos of the room.

Suddenly reminded of Dafna and Khanan's baby, René boomed, "How's Gilad?"

"*Doucement*," shushed Dafna. "He's fine. We'll take him for a stroll after the sun cools down. Coffee meanwhile?" We sat in a small garden until Dafna fetched eighteen-month-old Gilad, who blinked his large brown eyes in the still strong light. I marveled at the dominance of those eyes in yet another generation as Dafna strapped him onto her back.

"Let me show you the mayan," she said, filling me in on the history of the ancient water source in the center of the village. "Ein Kerem means 'well of the vineyards.' According to biblical myth, Mary, mother of Jesus, drew water at this very spot on her way to give birth in Bethlehem."

Over the millennia, the well had become a sacred site for Christian pilgrimages, eventually giving rise to the village that had existed here before 1948. Now Jewish inhabitants were rolling up their sleeves to rebuild the ruined homes with the help of small grants or low-cost loans from the Israeli government. Like Bar'am, the original Palestinian inhabitants would not be allowed back.

"You know," mused Dafna, "when you and Paula come back from France, you could have one of these houses too."

Across the valley, my gaze fell on a few forlorn-looking houses with caved-in roofs and broken walls, whose dark doors hung ajar like open mouths, their vacant windows gaping like ghostly eyes. A profound uneasiness came over me. What if the spirits of the previous owners were still lurking in the wreckage of their old homes? Had they fled (as the Israelis claimed) or been driven out (as the Palestinians insisted)? Try as I might, I couldn't reconcile these two conflicting narratives. I only knew in my bones that I'd never be able to make one of those abandoned homes my own.

Pondering this in silence, I tried to find joy in the unde-
niable charm of the village. But I wondered if René and Dafna
sensed my unease.

"Let me show you the monastery," Dafna continued. An
early evening breeze ruffled the trees as the sun sank below the
ridges. Long shafts of gold lit up their leaves. At the push of
an obscure black button, the monastery's massive iron doors
creaked open to reveal an otherworldly oasis. A paradise of
oleanders, olive trees, giant poplars, and conical firs spread out
below terra-cotta walls and towering turrets. The chime of bells
for evening vespers sent a few black-habited nuns gliding along
paths toward an inner sanctum.

Immune from human folly, peace reigned inside the
monastery's cloistered walls. Still, I had a hard time banishing
my thoughts of Ein Kerem's previous dwellers. Had the Jews
returned from two thousand years of exile only to oust another
people? Had fate reversed their roles, ousting those who had
lived here for generations in order for "new" refugees to rebuild
them? As the wheel of misfortune turned, some people would
always end up on the wrong side of history. Although I loved
the beauty of Ein Kerem, I couldn't silence the whisper in my
ears: *Would you welcome me back to my home if I returned from the
squalid refugee camp where I'm now condemned to live?*

But Israelis were not in a mood to be sentimental. Having
won the war, they had reclaimed what was rightfully theirs,
albeit after an absence of two thousand years. If innocent civilians had suffered, that was unfortunate, but their return posed
too great a risk. The only choice was to compartmentalize the
conflict and move forward with the building of the new state.

Jarring these thoughts, a pride of feral cats suddenly leapt
from a large open garbage bin near the bus stop, crossed our
path and disappeared just as quickly into trash-strewn thorn
bushes. Skinny and flea-bitten, their instinct for survival in such
harsh circumstances struck me as a metaphor for this part of the

world—a place where beauty, ugliness, resilience, and violence often overlapped. History here was complicated beyond my comprehension. Boundaries were forever shifting, justice fluctuated like a witching rod, and someone always seemed to get the short end of the stick. Were Dafna and Khanan to blame for making their home in a house whose original occupants could never return?

Returning to the house, René and Dafna lightened my mood with stories of their army escapades, over a pot of lemon verbena tea picked fresh from the vines on the *mirpeset*. Dafna had apparently done her basic training under the command of a Czech/Canadian sergeant, whose patience for his unruly female French charges had run thin. The harder he worked to transform them into soldiers, the more they goofed off and giggled; the heavier his punishments, the more they mocked him. When this sergeant came up for a promotion, Dafna and her girlfriends saw a chance to sabotage him. One night, on a mock reconnaissance mission, they ignored his orders to maintain strict silence. Instead of filling their canteens to the brim, they let the water slosh against the half-empty metal. Whining and whispering along the trail, they made extra stops to blow their noses and tighten their bootlaces. The sergeant had fumed furiously, but the damage was done. Unable to control his insubordinate troops, he received an unfavorable review the next day. The French girls' prank had cost him his promotion.

"What was his name?" I asked, laughing.

"Oh, you wouldn't know him," answered Dafna, but I persisted.

"Okay, okay," she paused. "I think he was called Gidon."

"Not Gidon Lev from Kibbutz Hazorea?" I echoed, incredulously.

"Why yes—how do you know him?"

"He just married my sister!" I gasped. "Oh my God, we're in-laws now."

"For better or worse," chuckled René.

Tears of laughter streamed down our cheeks as we realized the joke was now on us.

I didn't dare share this story with Gidon, but I hoped one day he and Dafna would fill their canteens with forgiveness. Despite the painful paradoxes of history, the village of Ein Kerem would become one of my favorite places in all of Israel. And despite the hilarious prank, I had a deep feeling that my friendship with Dafna would last a lifetime.

Church & Monastery in Ein Kerem

Paula and Dafna, A Lifelong Friendship, 2017

Chapter 35

PASSAGE TO FRANCE

By October of 1964, having said my farewells to all the people and places I'd come to love during my first year in Israel, I could no longer put off packing my few belongings for the final bus ride to Haifa. René wanted to reach France before the harsh Lyonnaise winter set in, and time was already short. His urgency made the last rays of the still-strong Mediterranean sun all the more precious. I could not imagine the cold, damp climate he described—a city under a blanket of frigid air on the banks of the Rhône and the Saône Rivers.

Anticipation fought with regret as I remembered all the tearful exoduses of my childhood as I left my schools and friends in Texas, Iowa, and Kansas on my parents' westward trek to California. Now as then, I soaked the sun's rays into every pore in a vain attempt to make my final days in Israel last forever.

We planned to spend our last night with Naomi and Gidon in Hazorea. With every bump on the rutted road south through the hills of Galilee, my pleasure in the landscape alternated with the pain of departure. When the bus made a lunch stop in Tiberias, I was relieved to follow the scent of falafel at the familiar outdoor stand where my family had enjoyed the vendor's juggling act as much as the food. René and I joined the line, our mouths watering like everyone else's. Placing my order, I savored the guttural sound of Hebrew, knowing I wouldn't hear it again for a long while.

The next morning at the dock in Haifa, Naomi and I hugged each other a final goodbye. My eyes welled up as her still-sleek belly pressed against mine, and my heart contracted, knowing that I'd miss the birth the following April. Life seemed to have run away with our plans. Even my penchant for planning hadn't foreseen this outcome. Maybe my mother was right when she said that life just happened to her.

Pulling away, I followed René up the ferry's waiting gangplank. Ferrying back and forth over the Mediterranean had become almost routine, yet this trip felt as momentous as my first journey to Israel. As the ship pulled away, Naomi and I waved until we could no longer see each other in the watery gap between shore and horizon. Yet as wrenching as this separation felt, I knew I could withstand it. Like a chameleon that grows its tail back after a sudden amputation, in the year of our initial separation, I had discovered the capacity to grow a new part of myself. The memory of chameleons' delicate resilience in the *kerem* was somehow comforting—the folds of their scaly rainbow skin and soft warm bodies palpable beneath my fingers.

I was truly leaving now. Naomi's mirror image played like a dark dot on the retina of my eye. But she was truly out of sight by now. Were her eyes as wet as mine or was she still keeping up the brave mask we'd learned to wear as children, like shields against the distress of leaving yet another home? Did she feel any surer than I of the life she had chosen—or the life that had chosen her? The pregnancy had forced her hand. I tried to look to the future, but my many trips to and from the port in Haifa spiraled before me like a gyroscope—my arrival in Israel in November of 1963; the trip to England and my family's brief but momentous visit to the Holy Land in the summer of '64—not to mention my Chanukah jaunt to Eilat or the move to Kibbutz Dan. No wonder my head was spinning and my heart brimming. With all its ups and downs, it had been one hell of a year of adventure! And France was still to come. As I'd done so many times before as a child, I released my grief and welcomed the excitement of a new journey.

Three days from now we'd arrive in Marseille, after which we'd board a train for Lyon, according to René who had taken care of the practical details of our itinerary. With my savings and the small kibbutz stipend almost gone, we had only enough to buy the ferry tickets and a few small gifts for René's family. But René had assured me his father would lend us the money for train tickets from Marseille to Lyon. I felt embarrassed to ask for help, but René was certain he could repay his dad as soon as he started working in the market. "Trust me," he said, and I had.

Thoughts of my mother waving goodbye to *her* mother flooded my mind, as they did with every departure. Had I learned from her example that to make a life with the man you loved meant sacrificing your own home and family? An indelible pattern of daughters leaving their mothers seemed imprinted in my DNA like the holy grail. Suddenly, I felt overwhelmed.

"I'm going below to rest," I told René.

Our third-class cabin felt familiar by now—barely wide enough for two bunks stacked on one side with a latched closet and a tiny washbasin on the other, and all too near the smelly toilets. Still, with the door closed, it felt like a sanctuary. Lying on the lower bunk, I watched the sunbeams refracting off the waves like water sprites in sparkling costumes dancing all over the cabin. Grateful to be neither refugee nor immigrant, I reminded myself that I had embarked on this new adventure of my own free will. Whatever the consequences, I was both captain of my ship and captive of my destiny. With that lofty thought, I fell into a trance, lulled by the lapping lullaby of waves. Soon I felt as weightless as a seagull's speckled feather floating on an ocean of history.

By the time I woke up, dinner was long over. But René had saved me a plate of tomato-cucumber salad, rice, and stringy meat from the mess hall. Balancing carefully, I mounted the metal staircase to the deck to enjoy my meal under the star-strewn sky. Glancing over the moonlit deck, I cocked my ears to make sure I was alone. Thankfully, no piercing cry of "Gingit!" rang out; and no randy sailor pounced out of the shadows on my passage to France.

With time temporarily suspended on those three days at sea, my thoughts spooled out like the wake of the ship. Tomorrow we would arrive in Marseille and my next adventure would begin.

Emboldened by my success in transforming my fantasy of Israel into reality, I had hatched an even grander scheme for the next ten years. After two or three years of working in France, René and I would have saved enough money to return to Israel where planned to settle in Jerusalem. I would attend the Hebrew University while René found a job or perhaps went to school as well. René had welcomed this plan, including my insistence that we return to Israel. After more than three years in the army, he too needed a new direction. Whatever twists and turns our French detour might entail, at least I felt sure of our common commitment on that score.

After France (if not before), I dreamed of starting a family. Although in the back of my mind, I wondered vaguely why it hadn't happened yet, especially with Naomi already expecting, I dismissed the shadow of my worries. If I could not foresee the future beyond my twenties, I believed with all my heart that a bright new vision would surely guide me to my next adventure.

As the ferry approached Marseille late in the last afternoon of our final day on the Mediterranean, the weather suddenly shifted from balmy to frigid. In a matter of minutes, the wind whipped the glassy calm to angry whitecaps. Lightning crackled in the gathering clouds, and sharp squalls lashed the deck. Undeterred, I stayed on deck to watch the city flicker into view in the stormy half-light. René wrapped me in his arms as I shivered in my flimsy summer clothes.

When the clouds parted briefly, I caught a glimpse of the evening star, shining through the storm like a talisman. "Look, Venus!" I shouted in the wind.

With the full momentum of youth driving me forward as inexorably as the wind now drove the ferry, what could possibly go wrong? With love, luck, and a lot of hard work, I felt sure I could overcome whatever obstacles lay ahead if only I followed my star. For the moment, my hopes held a victory party over my fears. Adventure had won the day! I took a deep breath, letting the brine rush into my throat. After the detour in France, I would have plenty of time to return to Israel as a newcomer in that ancient land.

Stormy Seas on the Mediterranean

ACKNOWLEDGMENTS

B oundless gratitude to my family, especially my husband, Gib, for his enduring love, infinite patience, and sense of humor as I burned the midnight oil; my cherished children and grandchildren, who light the way to the future but may also be curious about the past; my twin sister, Naomi, who corroborated facts and feelings but above all shares the laughter, tears, and love of our mutual journey. And to all my far-flung extended family, for enriching my world beyond my wildest dreams.

Heartfelt thanks to many friends and colleagues, including: Linda Joy Myers of the National Association of Memoir Writers (NAMW) for her tireless mentorship, encouragement, and faith as I slowly learned the art and craft of memoir writing; Brooke Warner, publisher par excellence of She Writes Press, for her forward vision, industry savvy, and fierce commitment to women writers; and my amazing in-person and online memoir community, too numerous to name, who critiqued and supported my early stories while inspiring me with theirs.

Special thanks to three friends: Victoria Post, my "other twin," whose spirit, insights, and lifelong friendship sustain me like lifeblood; Gail Williams, whose life exemplifies the meaning of persistence in the face of challenges; and Andi Stein, for making fun her motto in life!

Sincere appreciation to The Story Circle Network Conference in Austin, TX, for the magic that happens when women writers gather together; kudos to web designer Sam Baja for her delightful creativity and formidable tech skills; a big shout-out to Crystal Patriarche of BookSparks for her energy in marketing the muse; and finally, a huge surge of gratitude to my readers!

You have all taught me that bringing a book to life takes a village. Your caring support has helped transform the sometimes lonely slog of writing into a joyful mission. For these and many more blessings, I am forever grateful.

ABOUT THE AUTHOR

Paula Wagner and her twin sister were born in London to an English mother and a Jewish-American father. Arriving in the US, they grew up moving across the South and Midwest before the family finally settled in Northern California. Enticed by wanderlust at an early age, Paula has also lived in Israel, Italy, and France. She holds a master's in career development and a BA in women's studies, and has studied languages at the Hebrew University of Jerusalem. She divides her time between creative writing and career coaching. She and her husband currently live in Albany, CA. Their blended family includes four children, eight grandkids, and an extended family worldwide. Besides writing, Paula enjoys travel, swimming, singing, hiking, biking, river rafting, yoga, cooking, and building community.

Author photo © Raymond Holbert, MemoryBank Images

SELECTED TITLES FROM SHE WRITES PRESS

She Writes Press is an independent publishing company founded to serve women writers everywhere. Visit us at www.shewritespress.com.

Accidental Soldier: A Memoir of Service and Sacrifice in the Israel Defense Forces by Dorit Sasson. $17.95, 978-1-63152-035-8. When nineteen-year-old Dorit Sasson realized she had no choice but to distance herself from her neurotic, worrywart of a mother in order to become her own person, she volunteered for the Israel Defense Forces—and found her path to freedom.

Home Free: Adventures of a Child of the Sixties by Rifka Kreiter. $16.95, 978-1631521768. A memoir of a young woman's passionate quest for liberation—one that leads her out of the darkness of a fraught childhood and through Manhattan nightclubs, broken love affairs, and virtually all the political and spiritual movements of the sixties.

You Can't Buy Love Like That: Growing Up Gay in the Sixties by Carol E. Anderson. $16.95, 978-1631523144. A young lesbian girl grows beyond fear to fearlessness as she comes of age in the '60s amid religious, social, and legal barriers.

Peanut Butter and Naan: Stories of an American Mother in The Far East by Jennifer Magnuson. $16.95, 978-1-63152-911-5. The hilarious tale of what happened when Jennifer Magnuson moved her family of seven from Nashville to India in an effort to shake things up—and got more than she bargained for.

Gap Year Girl by Marianne Bohr. $16.95, 978-1-63152-820-0. Thirty-plus years after first backpacking through Europe, Marianne Bohr and her husband leave their lives behind and take off on a yearlong quest for adventure.

This is Mexico: Tales of Culture and Other Complications by Carol M. Merchasin. $16.95, 978-1-63152-962-7. Merchasin chronicles her attempts to understand Mexico, her adopted country, through improbable situations and small moments that keep the reader moving between laughter and tears.

CPSIA information can be obtained
at www.ICGtesting.com
Printed in the USA
FSHW021747070419
57040FS

2 370000 677037